821.008
DOO

City and Islington Sixth Form College
283-309 Goswell Road
London
EC1V 7LA
020 7520 0652

KT-426-660

CITY AND ISLINGTON
COLLEGE

IGTON

This book is due for return on or before the date last stamped below.
You may renew by telephone. Please quote the Barcode No.
May not be renewed if required by another reader.

Fine: 5p per day

1 0 JUN 2008

0 1 JUL 2008

City & Islington College

SA014993

MAURA DOOLEY was born in Truro, grew up in Bristol, and after some years in Yorkshire now lives in London. Both her first two collections have been Poetry Book Society Recommendations: *Explaining Magnetism* (1991) and *Kissing a Bone* (1996), both published by Bloodaxe, and *Kissing a Bone* was shortlisted for the T.S. Eliot Prize. Her latest books are *How Novelists Work*, published by Seren in 2000, and her anthology *The Honey Gatherers: Love Poems*, due from Bloodaxe in 2002. ●

SA014993

Making for Planet Alice

NEW WOMEN POETS

EDITED BY MAURA DOOLEY

BLOODAXE BOOKS

Copyright © Bloodaxe Books Ltd 1997.
Selection and introduction copyright © Maura Dooley 1997.
Copyright of poems resides with authors as listed.

ISBN: 1 85224 398 8

First published 1997 by
Bloodaxe Books Ltd,
Highgreen,
Tarset,
Northumberland NE48 1RP.

Bloodaxe Books Ltd acknowledges
the financial assistance of Northern Arts.

northern
arts

LEGAL NOTICE

All rights reserved. No part of this book may be
reproduced, stored in a retrieval system, or
transmitted in any form, or by any means, electronic,
mechanical, photocopying, recording or otherwise,
without prior written permission from Bloodaxe Books Ltd
or from the copyright holders listed on page 6.

Requests to publish work from this book must be
sent to the copyright holders listed on page 6.

Second impression 2001.

Cover printing by J. Thomson Colour Printers Ltd, Glasgow.

Printed in Great Britain by
Cromwell Press Ltd, Trowbridge, Wiltshire.

for my mother

'The purpose of poetry is to remind us
how difficult it is to remain just one person,
for our house is open, there are no keys in the door,
and invisible guests come in and out at will.'

CZESLAW MILOSZ
(translated by the author & Lillian Vallee)

Acknowledgements

Acknowledgements are due to the authors and to the publishers of these books from which poems have been selected for this anthology:

Blackstaff Press Ltd: Siobhán Campbell, *The Permanent Wave* (1996).

Bloodaxe Books Ltd: Moniza Alvi, *Carrying My Wife* (2000), including *The Country at My Shoulder* (1993), *A Bowl of Warm Air* (1996); Eleanor Brown, *Maiden Speech* (1996); Julia Copus, *The Shuttered Eye* (1995); Gillian Ferguson, *Air for Sleeping Fish* (1997); Linda France, *Red* (1992), *The Gentleness of the Very Tall* (1994), *Storyville* (1997); Elizabeth Garrett, *The Rule of Three* (1991), *A Two-Part Invention* (1998); Maggie Hannan, *Liar, Jones* (1995); Tracey Herd, *No Hiding Place* (1996); Jane Holland, *The Brief History of a Disreputable Woman* (1997); Jackie Kay, *The Adoption Papers* (1991), *Other Lovers* (1993); Gwyneth Lewis, *Parables & Faxes* (1995); Ruth Padel, *Angel* (1993); Anne Rouse, *Sunset Grill* (1993), *Timing* (1997); Eva Salzman, *The English Earthquake* (1992); Ann Sansom, *Romance* (1994).

Carcanet Press Ltd: Sophie Hannah, *The Hero and the Girl Next Door* (1995), *Hotels like Houses* (1996); Mimi Khalvati, *In White Ink* (1991), *Mirrorwork* (1995); Sinéad Morrissey, *There was Fire in Vancouver* (1996).

Enitharmon Press: Jane Duran, *Breathe Now, Breathe* (1995).

Faber & Faber Ltd: Lavinia Greenlaw, *Night Photograph* (1993); Katherine Pierpoint, *Truffle Beds* (1995); Susan Wicks, *Singing Underwater* (1992), *Open Diagnosis* (1994), *The Clever Daughter* (1996).

The Gallery Press: Vona Groarke, *Shale* (1994).

Oxford University Press: Tessa Rose Chester, *Provisions of Light* (1996); Alice Oswald, *The Thing in the Gap-Stone Stile* (1996); Eva Salzman, *Bargain with the Watchman* (1997).

Random House UK Ltd, for books published by Chatto & Windus Ltd: Kate Clanchy, *Slattern* (1996); Ruth Padel, *Fusewire* (1996).

Janet Fisher for work from *Listening to Dancing* (Smith/Doorstop Books, 1996); **Lavinia Greenlaw, Jackie Kay** and **Gwyneth Lewis** for new poems; **Sarah Maguire** for work from *Spilt Milk* (Secker & Warburg, 1991) and *The Invisible Mender* (Jonathan Cape, 1997); **Ruth Padel** for work first published in *Summer Snow* (Hutchinson, 1990) and the *London Review of Books*; **Deryn Rees-Jones** for work from *The Memory Tray* (Seren Books, 1994) and *Signs Round a Dead Body* (Seren, 1998).

Permission to further reprint or reproduce poems from *Making for Planet Alice* should be sought from the copyright holders listed above (not from Bloodaxe Books except in the case of collections published by Bloodaxe Books).

Contents

Introduction

Making for Planet Alice follows a line of anthologies of women's work, beginning in the late 1970s with *One Foot on the Mountain*, edited by Lillian Mohin. Many of these books have been, have had to be, pioneering political collections and have made a significant contribution to the changing status of poetry by women. So that, by the time Bloodaxe's *Sixty Women Poets* came to be published in 1993, it did seem possible to rejoice with editor Linda France in 'women being positive, creative and in control of their own lives'. Yet when I was asked to put together this anthology one of my first thoughts was 'another anthology of women poets? Not again, not now, surely not?' The thought ran more or less in parallel with my certainty that the first half of this decade has seen an upsurge of good new poets and that most of them are women. I did not want to contemplate an anthology that might exclude the male reader, creating a separate culture for the writers included. Was there need enough of an anthology simply to celebrate them? I rehearsed to myself the familiar debate.

The old argument sets poets who happen to be women in an unhappy groove of ambivalence. The argument runs like this. Women no longer have the same struggle to be published: their work is bought, borrowed and read, heard on radio and at public readings. To continue to publish and promote them separately is to create a literary ghetto or a cultural sideshow. The counter argument runs like this. Women are published, read and heard, but their work is not discussed. Until their work is considered and written about consistently, seriously and undifferentiatingly by the major literary journals of the day, their poetry will not have a future as part of the main canon of English Literature. Enough will not have been said about the poems to secure them a lasting readership.

More than twenty years ago, in her introduction to *The World Split Open*, one of the first anthologies of women's poetry to be published in this country, Louise Bernikow writes: 'Which writers have survived their time and which have not depends upon who noticed them and chose to record the notice.' Collections of poetry by women continue to be bundled up and reviewed together by some journals, as if their gender gave them something in common, something more, that is, than deserving only one eighth of the space given by the same journal to a single collection by a male poet.

There was a time when the word 'domestic' occurred to good effect, like a reflex, in any review of a new collection by a woman, thereby relegating both scope of book and scope of ambition to the kitchen. Write about blood, babies, the moon and jam-making and be a 'Woman Poet'; or, cut out half of your experience of life and get taken seriously. Maybe. Now, however, we are led to believe that all such problematic stereotyping has been swept away, thanks to the purposeful strides of women poets of the 1970s and 1980s, thanks to the rehabilitation of some lost poets of earlier decades such as Anna Wickham, Ruth Pitter, Laura Riding, E.J. Scovell, thanks to the sheer slog of the women's presses, the enlightened work of a few of the mainstream poetry presses (and the oppor-tunist work of others), and, finally, thanks to a landslide of excel-lent and invigorating new poetry by women. This evolution, it is suggested, has even made it possible for men to chart some of these dangerous seas themselves: Maurice Riordan, Andrew Motion and Robert Crawford have all done so skilfully and avoided the *we hurt too* school of male post-feminist writing.

Yet I see the bold linguistic playfulness of Maggie Hannan or Gwyneth Lewis, the irony of Kate Clanchy or Sophie Hannah, the intellectual rigour of Ruth Padel or Lavinia Greenlaw, the for-mal authority of Elizabeth Garrett or Alice Oswald, the imagina-tive reach of Jackie Kay and Deryn Rees-Jones, too little recorded and too often overlooked in any attempts in essays, discursive reviews or recent critical appraisals to convey the true flavour of what's happening in current poetry.

The defining principle of this anthology has been to bring to-gether thirty poets, each of whom has published her first collec-tion since 1990, some already well-known and established, others just in print. In selecting the poems I have tried to give some sense of the breadth and diversity of these poets. So fruitful has this decade been that I wish there had been room for another ten poets whose work I admire but simply could not fit in. It's the anthologiser's lament that hard choices have to be made but I hear their ghost voices as a rebuke within these pages.

Women gathering their thoughts in the 1980s and their laurels in the 1990s have been able to embrace both Modernism and Post-modernism and take from them what they choose. Where post-modernist manners have sometimes stultified the novel into a series of attitudes, those same many-peopled, many-faceted perspectives have usefully quaked the earth beneath the feet of the contempo-rary poetry reader.

These are poets who have grown up secure not only with Sylvia Plath, Elizabeth Bishop, Stevie Smith and Elizabeth Jennings but with a growing confidence in a tumultuous family tree as likely to include Jean Binta Breeze as Wendy Mulford, Anna Akhmatova as Wendy Cope. Behind the work of these thirty stand Anne Stevenson, Eavan Boland, U.A. Fanthorpe, Medbh McGuckian, Grace Nichols, Fleur Adcock, Selima Hill, Liz Lochhead, Gillian Clarke, Sharon Olds, Carol Rumens, Denise Riley, Jo Shapcott, Sujata Bhatt, Carol Ann Duffy and too many more to mention here, all of whom have helped create the current happy climate for women writing, reading and publishing today. Here are poets of the moment, inheritors, who seem to me to be responding to the shadowy closing years of this century with an energy, vigour, inventiveness and intelligence fit for the next. In the first anthology of women's poetry to be published in this country, in 1979, women were allowed to set *One Foot on the Mountain*. The poets in this anthology are *Making for Planet Alice*.

It has become fashionable for anthologies to announce and identify themselves through polemic. Reviewers are often rightly delighted to find a vision or an argument with which they can run and with which the letters column can reverberate for weeks. Yet the point of these anthologies is surely the contents, the poems themselves. My single hope for this anthology is that the reviewer will read and discuss the poems as well as engage in the politics of editing. I *know* the general reader will.

MAURA DOOLEY

Moniza Alvi

MONIZA ALVI grew up in Britain but was born in Pakistan. Her experience of those two very different countries and cultures creates many of the joys and tensions explored in her poetry. Her work is vivid, witty and imbued with unexpected and delicious glimpses of the surreal – this poet's third country. Moniza Alvi was chosen to be part of the New Generation promotion in 1994 and her first book was a Poetry Book Society Recommendation. She works as a teacher and lives in South West London. ●

Selection from: *Carrying My Wife* (2000 Bloodaxe), from *The Country at My Shoulder* (1993) and *A Bowl of Warm Air* (1996).

The Laughing Moon

I had two pillows and one was England,
two cheeks and one was England.

Pakistan held me and dropped me in the night.
I slid through
        yesterday and tomorrow –

An unknown country crept between
my toes, threw an ocean behind my eye.
I couldn't tell whether the sky was red
or green, cotton or silk and if it would tear.

I could see myself spinning like an important
message through a hole to the other side
        of the world.

I'd held out my arms to kingfishers and tigers,
I'd sipped each moment like a language,
touched something I knew better
than my own parcel-weight.

Shakily England picked me up
        with her grey fingers.
England had a cure for everything
stuck between the bricks of houses.

The continents were very old,
but I was new and breathing in
        midnight,

the laughing moon in its place.

Houdini

It is not clear how he entered me
or why he always has to escape.
Maybe he's just proving to the crowds
he can still do it – He whispers
half-words which bloom in the dark
Ma ha ma ha.

Sometimes he feeds me cough medicine.
Or bathes his genitals in salt water.
Then heaves his body upwards
as if pressing against a lid.
At least he prefers me
to his underwater box, to the manacles
which clank on his moon-white skin.
I wonder what it is exactly
he sees within me?
He touches my insides as though
he'd sighted the first landplants –
I'm catching cloud between my fingers.

Tonight the wind whips through my stomach
over knots of trees and sharp rocks.
When he rushes out of me the crowd gasps –
and I implode from sheer emptiness.

Presents from My Aunts in Pakistan

They sent me a salwar kameez
                    peacock-blue,
                              and another
          glistening like an orange split open,
embossed slippers, gold and black
                    points curling.
          Candy-striped glass bangles
                    snapped, drew blood.
          Like at school, fashions changed
                    in Pakistan –
the salwar bottoms were broad and stiff,
                    then narrow.
My aunts chose an apple-green sari,
          silver-bordered
                    for my teens.

I tried each satin-silken top –
          was alien in the sitting-room.
I could never be as lovely
                    as those clothes –
          I longed
for denim and corduroy.
          My costume clung to me
                    and I was aflame,
I couldn't rise up out of its fire,
          half-English,
                    unlike Aunt Jamila.

I wanted my parents' camel-skin lamp –
          switching it on in my bedroom,
to consider the cruelty
                    and the transformation
from camel to shade,
          marvel at the colours
                    like stained glass.

My mother cherished her jewellery –
    Indian gold, dangling, filigree.
        But it was stolen from our car.
The presents were radiant in my wardrobe.
    My aunts requested cardigans
        from Marks and Spencers.

My salwar kameez
    didn't impress the schoolfriend
who sat on my bed, asked to see
    my weekend clothes.
But often I admired the mirror-work,
    tried to glimpse myself
        in the miniature
glass circles, recall the story
    how the three of us
        sailed to England.
Prickly heat had me screaming on the way.
    I ended up in a cot
in my English grandmother's dining-room,
    found myself alone,
        playing with a tin boat.

I pictured my birthplace
    from fifties' photographs.
        When I was older
there was conflict, a fractured land
    throbbing through newsprint.
Sometimes I saw Lahore –
        my aunts in shaded rooms,
screened from male visitors,
    sorting presents,
        wrapping them in tissue.

Or there were beggars, sweeper-girls
    and I was there –
        of no fixed nationality,
staring through fretwork
        at the Shalimar Gardens.

The Bed

We have travelled many miles to find this bed,
scanned tedious columns of small print,
waited in queues at bus stops.
And now we think we have it –

But we'll have to get it home –
no one can deliver it for us.

We must test it.

Is it wide enough for a family?
Will it hold the tempests of our dreams?

And when we are accustomed to it,
when the pillows burst their stomachs
and ecstatic feathers fly towards the cornice,
then perhaps, we'll have that river
in the middle of the bed –

Where in the ancient song
the King's horses could all drink together.

Eleanor Brown

ELEANOR BROWN was born in 1969 in England but grew up in Scotland. She studied English at York University, took temporary jobs in hotels and bars and then travelled in France where she lived for a while in a convent. Similarly enjoyable juxtapositions are at work in the poems of this witty, sophisticated writer who handles rhythm and rhyme, the men and the boys, with equal assurance. Eleanor Brown won an Eric Gregory Award in 1993. She lives in Hertfordshire where she works as a barmaid. ●

Selection from: *Maiden Speech* (1996 Bloodaxe).

Bitcherel

You ask what I think of your new acquisition;
and since we are now to be 'friends',
I'll strive to the full to cement my position
with honesty. Dear – it depends.

It depends upon taste, which must not be disputed;
for which of us *does* understand
why some like their furnishings pallid and muted,
their cookery wholesome, but bland?

There isn't a *law* that a face should have features,
it's just that they generally *do*;
God couldn't give colour to *all* of his creatures,
and only gave wit to a few;

I'm sure she has qualities, much underrated,
that compensate amply for this,
along with a charm that is so understated
it's easy for people to miss.

And if there are some who choose clothing to flatter
what beauties they think they possess,
when what's underneath has no shape, does it matter
if there is no shape to the dress?

It's not that I think she is *boring*, precisely,
that isn't the word I would choose;
I know there are men who like girls who talk nicely
and always wear sensible shoes.

It's not that I think she is vapid and silly;
it's not that her voice makes me wince;
but – chilli con carne without any chilli
is only a plateful of mince...

Jezebel to the Eunuchs

No priests. No tiring-women. If you please,
no pity, though I don't object to fear.
Furthermore, absolutely no
prophets, croaking 'I told you so.'
Lock up this turret room; give me the keys.
Vengeance can bloody come and get me here.
No prayers, reproaches, tears or homilies.
You three are privileged, you realise?
Marred men, whom nobody can mend,
you'll see how greatness makes its end –
even take part. You place your sympathies
where you want to; your Queen accepts she dies
in any case. You see that cloud of dust?
That's Jehu, driving like a lunatic.
Poor, god-pecked Jehu, comes to close
my wicked mouth for good. Ah, those
Jews, majestic tools of Yahweh! It must –
I can't believe it doesn't ever stick
in their throats, to grovel for such a god.
Pathetically obsessed with cleanliness,
their god. Well, just in case I meet
him: perfumed oil, to make me sweet
(no time for a bath now). You think this odd?
You'd dress for dinner, but you wouldn't dress
for death? I'll be prepared. Rouge, now, and kohl.

That smaller brush. Death: the greatest and last
of any woman's appointments –
surely the usual ointments
are not out of place – she should stay in rôle,
for fear of seeming to regret her past.
All past, the 'whoredoms, witchcrafts', sins and snares,
abominable to God. Or so they tell
me. Is he here yet? At the gate?
Oh, Jehu, Jehu – just too late.
Vengeance, that thinks to take me unawares
finds me ready, and looking…rather well.

Out

Strip her first of home and family;
erase surname and address.
Second, dismantle national identity;
take away passport, language and race memory,
if any.
Leave her the clothes she stands
up in, and a little black dress –
indispensable, haw haw. No, no – not a penny.
Take off the blindfold; untie her hands.

Your name is no name.
You are no one's daughter, sister or wife.
No friend wonders where you are;
no lover dreams of you at night.
No, we can't help you. This is not a game;
it's a serious business, all right?
Never heard of it. No idea how far.
Really? What a shame.
Still, that's life.

One moment, miss.
Before we leave you, a quick check
to make sure the job's been done
thoroughly. Do you recognise this?

Or this? Do you rec-
ognise any of the following names: Christ,
Shakespeare, Beethoven, Rembrandt? None?
Excellent. Do you know what 'Zeitgeist'
means? The sun:

does it orbit the earth, or vice versa?
What is the penalty
for breaking the law of gravity?
What is the difference between Asia and Ursa
Minor?
Who wrote Montaigne's Essays? Where
is Mother Nature's vagina?
Can you name one famous fashion designer?
All right, gentlemen, I think we can leave it there.

Tragic Hero

Self-styled reluctant womaniser; less
predator, he, than lost-boy-victim, yes?
Touchingly hesitant, he, to confess
that all his life he has been in a mess;

meanwhile, his gentle, adept eyes assess
the fastenings and workings of her dress.

And after her? Another her, to bless
his cotton socks, to soothe his loneliness,
to kiss his melancholy lips, to press
her undistinguished gift of a caress
upon him, whose high-seeming, strange distress

is permanent post-coital tristesse.

Sonnet XLIII

He is a very inoffensive man;
a man without grave faults or dreadful tastes,
who need not be embarrassing; who can
tell an amusing anecdote; who wastes
less time than most on foolish flattery,
without descending into boorishness;
can pay a compliment quite prettily,
avoiding many kinds of clumsiness;
a very inoffensive man indeed;
an interesting man, and sensitive;
the sort that would be pleased to soothe a need,
if it were anything that he could give;
and I have sat with him this whole day through,
and hated him, because he is not you.

What Song the Syrens Sang

I genuinely wanted them to come.
It's most important that you understand
there was no malice in it. Only loss,
each time, and every time the loss was mine.
How could it have succeeded, otherwise?
Who embraces death on the strength of some
lukewarm invitation? No bald command,
no whore's cold patter gets a man to toss
his life away. Accident, not design,
flooded and burst their lungs; I sang no lies.

I never lied. I told them what I'd done,
each time. But who was listening to me?
I pointed out my island's grisly necklace
of wave-washed bones; sometimes I even cried,
sincerely, urgently, please, do not come!

On the knife horizon, the evening sun
slit his own throat and bled into the sea,
while they, the foolish, fascinated reckless,
jumped in to drown. I watched them as they died,
praying to all the gods to strike me dumb.

You understand, I had a job to do.
I did it very well – which doesn't mean
that I was ever satisfied. It was
no joy to me to see what I desired
struggle, fail, die, drift too late to my shore.
Why should I bother saying this to you?
Because in all my life I've never been
heard, when I warned 'I'm trouble.' Or because
I want you not to come to me. I'm tired.
I do not want to do this any more.

Siobhán Campbell

SIOBHÁN CAMPBELL was born in 1962 in Dublin, where she still lives, and where she was also educated. She has worked in publishing and taken part in various writers' workshops in that city. In 1992 she lived in New York, performing her work at the Nuyorican Poets Café and at Sin É. Her poetry uses sensuous narrative to explore the surprising, wry, hidden stories that make up our lives. She has been widely published in journals and anthologies. She is married with one daughter. ●

Selection from: *The Permanent Wave* (1996 Blackstaff Press).

The Chairmaker

I have been tempted to rush the job –
to cut, not shave; to glue, not join,
but when I stand beside it
and it's a friend or when I sit astride
and it's solid as a past, then I know
I am right to bide my time.

When people ask me how, I say
'My lady knows, she bakes loaves of bread.'
I tried that too until she said
if I kept opening the oven door
her rise would fall.

So I went back out to my shed
and dreamt myself a piece of elm.
I watched its wave and fingered the swell
and started to work slow as you like
letting my bevel follow the grain.

But this straight back kept coming up long,
thinned as it came until almost a pole.
I kept going although it was strange,
honing the shaft and slatting the seat
which was high and tiny and more like a tray.

She came to me when the loaves were done
as if to make up for forcing me out.
She looked at it and her eyes were lit,
'A bird table! We can put it outside,
sit on your chairs and watch them sing.'
And eat your bread, I said (I felt obliged),
and that night was as good as it's ever been.

Big John's Tears Fall to the River

You would always offer me a mug
hating the way my fingers surrounded your china.
You knew that being a cliché already
there was nothing to be done.
I wanted to tell you of my growing,
of that sudden sighting in the mirror –
but I am of this creature
and must love him for shelter.

In this town they don't expect to hear me speak
assuming some sort of generous simplicity
and you left because I failed to speak.
Now I am folded in lumbering despair.
Sometimes I wonder
did God have a hand in me at all
or was I fashioned
to make others raise a prayer?

Legacy

I

Going north meant Opal Fruits and Aztec bars,
things we couldn't get down south,
the thrill of secret cameras at the border
and the smell of ham in my grandmother's house.

Dad would skip tea, sitting in the car
where I ran once to get away from china dogs;
a shuffle of magazines into a paper bag –
had I really seen a bare bum in a tyre?

Later when I found them in his bedside drawer,
stories of caning set in schools or parties where
girls were made perform, my wetness drew me
and following the rhythms, I learned how to move.
Soon I knew *Playboy* had too much text on cars,
Hustler was more daring, written to arouse; two men,
one woman or the innocent's new job,
who will have her, she's wide open for the taking.

II

I took my fantasies from what you chose,
*Schoolgirl Susan Spanking, Debbie All Alone
in Summer*. I felt the hold of the observing eye
and learned the tone of the intimate narrator.
Lying on your bed, one ear attuned to anyone
returning home, I found new words for things
I had not seen; spunk and cock, jism and cum,
clit was a place I was not sure I'd been.

Weeks of waiting after you'd been north
would culminate in finding what you'd brought.
By now I could create a froth, summon
a spring, dive a deep river in my brain.
These rhythms I had learned to sing:
cunt becomes liquid, lips I have four,
my mouth devouring, nipples stand and stare,
the lightest flick from a wet finger and I'm there.

III

Then you produced a cutting on the white slave
trade to chasten me before I left for France.
On the back was a sliver of brown leg.
Here was headlined 'harems for sheiks
where young girls are kept against their will'.

Did the rest go on to make their abuse a thrill?
You saw that I knew what it was from.
You'd blown your cover in order to warn.

I left your drawer alone but what I read survived.
The cool onlooker through the two-way mirror
still arrives to speed my loving on as if
I'll never have the time. I want to shut it down,
to be wordless in my wonder or dream a new
theme from my own gender. But it's too late.
These riffs by now are mine. You helped to make
the lover I became. I am what you and I have known.

The Constant Welcome

The constant welcome floors me.
I live here. I have arrived.
Yet still you cream me
with that smile.

I do not fight,
you'd twist my words to please.
I cannot go,
you'd follow if I leave.

But daughter,
do you know what I can hear
when your eyes are widening
as they want to close?

I can hear
the little scrape of hate
edging the high notes
of your voice.

Tessa Rose Chester

EADEN LILLEY

TESSA ROSE CHESTER was born in 1950 in London. After starting a foundation course at Harrow Art College, she married and moved to Cambridge where her children grew up. She later studied librarianship and began reading and writing poetry again in the 1990s. Her work shows formal alacrity, an ability to summon such precise images that we shiver with her in a wintry English landscape. Tessa Rose Chester is Curator of Children's Books at Bethnal Green Museum of Childhood, London. ●

Selection from: *Provisions of Light* (1996 OUP).

A Candle at Canterbury
(for Muriel)

1 *Rye harbour, night*

Marshland merges with a tarry sea.
A long, thin road bleeds into the sky,
the only life-line on a palm empty

of all promise. I stand, terrified.
The infinite depth, the infinite height
of blackness, with its sole unblinking eye

The Fisherman's Rest, burning through a night
I never wanted to confront alone.
Yet here I am. I keep the car in sight

and call my mother from the public phone
whose solid presence strangely dignifies
my fear, makes it respectable. Her tone

of voice confirms a death. So: yet more ties
with childhood cut. Perhaps the distant scenes
I can recall will serve to exorcise

my blurred, unfamiliar aunt. I have jeans
and grass-stained trainers, odd socks, anorak.
I don't have either will or extra means

to purchase petrol, or funereal black.
She says there is no need to come: somehow
I feel quite uninvolved; the slap and tack

of water thickening on an unseen bow
is all I hear, that matters, anyhow.

2 *Canterbury*

Passing down the great cathedral's throat
I shift the dark. A cough of shadows
is released and in slow motion floats

about a gasp of nuns and widows
sunk upon their polished agate knees,
impressive in this genuflecting pose;

even dust clouds sparkle with their pleas,
illuminating prayers in blue and gold.
I stand aloof. What's this to do with me,

an atheist for years; my god grew old
and withered when my father died. But here,
watching all these pilgrims newly souled,

I turn towards the sputtering bank and clear
a space; take a candle; speak a name;
set light within a hundred lights, a bier

of incandescent holy-water flame.
We sit, the dead and I. There is no blame.

3 *Rye harbour, dawn*

It's the last, the very last place on earth
to want to be. I find the pub asleep,
the same huge stillness waiting for the birth

of sound. Even the solitary gull keeps
counsel as he wheels once then dips again,
a little boat beached well within his sweep.

Funerals are not my scene; since the rain
drowned my father's January flowers
and drained his cards of our final words; pain

made worse by undiscriminating showers.
Families are so much rotten news;
at least, I can't explain the strain in ours.

My given name is all I have to lose.
I find it, suddenly, on hull and sail
of this small boat. It's a sign, but on whose

side? At this low ebb of mine, on this pale
beach, is there, have I still time to fail?

Buttons

Appointment on a rainy afternoon:
a way to heal relationships, he said.
She felt like drowning in the fluid gloom;

this was worse than anything she'd read.
He told them to relax; brought out a box;
explained the button game. Removed the lid.

At once I'm kneeling by a fire, my socks
alive with twitchy sparks. Gritty grains
of coal scratch my legs, hidden in the flock

of great-grandmother's rug. The window-panes
creak with frost. My mother sews above
me, talking on and off. She has to crane

her neck to see how I am. It's enough
just to be part of this transient thumbnail
scene. I warm my toes. She darns her glove.

Through my fingers buttons click like hail:
a steel sonata for the avant-garde,
a trickling glockenspiel, an echoing bell.

Glazy eyes cast rainbows, delicately starred.
I stroke their bones with my thumb: fabric flutes
and gills, some marble-smooth, some ribbed and barred.

Buttons fill small hands. Jade-green balls, coot-
black beads, globules of watery glass,
purple berries, tarnished moons in pewter-

grey, tiny plastic red and yellow hearts.
I lay them out as offerings around
my mother's feet. Fragile cameos, brass

pennies, copper clover-leaves, pearl fish wound
about with faded thread. Row on row
encircling us. Strange how trivial things resound

with vibes, percussive magic deep and slow.
Sorting buttons into lives, making sense
of self through patterning. Now I know.

She makes her choice. He cannot recompense
her for lost years, there's nothing to retrieve.
Rising, buttons spill, but she's caught the scent

of freshened futures. So much to achieve
without old ties! There'll be no time to grieve.

At 'Relate', couples may be asked to choose the buttons
they think most resemble each other.

Running Hares
A Winter Convalescence

These clothes don't fit.
You packed odd socks, tatty pants;
pale stains from a previous flesh.

Trust you to get it wrong.
I want things new
to comfort vulnerable skin.

Not that I look that different,
you understand,
but deep inside

past all the little gates
of knitted silk,
I'm freshly pruned and strung,

cut like the wind
that shapes the fen
where I walk each day

with only the low red sun
to see, and hares
running in the snow.

Kate Clanchy

JONATHAN McCREE

KATE CLANCHY was born in Glasgow in 1965 and educated in Edinburgh and Oxford. Her poems are fresh, ironic, lyrical and defiant. The muse, she has said, is desire, and she writes about desire 'just as men always have ... proclaiming, seducing, reproaching, all of it out loud'. Kate Clanchy won a Gregory Award in 1994. *Slattern* was a Poetry Book Society Recommendation, and won the Forward Prize for Best First Collection and the Saltire Society Scottish First Book of the Year Award in 1996. She works as a teacher and lives in the East End of London. ●

Selection from: *Slattern* (1996 Chatto).

Recognition

Either my sight is getting worse,
or everyone looks like somebody else.
A trick of the light, perhaps, or shadows

in this dark bar with its fancy candles,
but I think the girl in hippy sandals
could turn, and in a spin of bangles,

be a girl I know but somehow younger,
her before I even knew her.
Or the skinny boy in the Aran jumper,

hair in the nape of his neck like a feather,
could puff out smoke, be my first lover
pulling me, laughing, into the shower:

as if no one I knew had ever got older,
haircuts, glasses, or just wandered further
than I could follow, chose to bother;

as if through sheer short-sightedness,
I could recover, rewrite losses,
sift through face on face-like faces,

make one focus, crystallise,
pull towards me, recognise,
see themselves, once more, in my blue eyes.

Foreign

Consider abroad, how closely it brushes,
stiffens your skin like the scaly paw
of a fake fur throw when you wake at four
in a cheap hotel; creeps in sly as the hand
up your thigh on the spiralling, narrowing
minaret steps, clammy and moist as the stump
of a limb that's round as a baseball bat
but soft as the skin on the pad of cats' paws.

Think of the smells, the insecticide soaked
through your rucksack, passport; the rubbery
mould on the inside of tents; the medieval streets
with their stink like a phone box; the rain
on the dust, that stench of damp dog; the rush
of iron fresh from the butcher's; the stale
of the coppery water in temples, yellow-
ringed puddles behind great beaten doors.

And noises, the multiple clicks in your mind
like a camera; the howling of prayers
tannoyed from towers; the orders,
the bargains, the beggar's *baksheesh*; flip
flop flip of doors on buses; shrieks
from quarrels you can't understand,
buzzes and flies, the sound of the crowd
rising like water left running for hours.

Above all remember how little this touches,
how by evening it's telly, just small people
miming their hunger and rage. Remember,
against the prospect of mountains, the slice

of a city glimpsed through a window,
to measure that peering in mirrors for sun tans,
those glances in darkened windows of coaches,
searching your face for the difference.

One Night When We Paused Half-way

I saw you naked, gazing past me,
your face drawn tight and narrow
as if straining in harsh sun,

as if standing at some crossroads
surveying faceless fields of wheat.
One hand on the humming motor

counting the strung-out poles from home.

Deadman's Shoes

Last night your ghost walked in at two,
tall, calm as a father with his evening drink,
turned his back and sat to peel one sock off,
then the other. I hardly stirred, just matched
your usual sigh to my own intake of breath,
and slept on, near you, comforted;

but woke late and looked for your shoes
dropped in first position on the carpet.
The deadman's brogues we bought
that day in Brighton, inners stamped
with the outline of an instep. I wanted,
very much, to put my hands inside them.

For a Wedding
(Camilla and Kieran 9/8/94)

Cousin, I think the shape of a marriage
is like the shelves my parents have carried
through Scotland to London, three houses;

is not distinguished, fine, French-polished,
but plywood and tatty, made
in the first place for children to batter,

still carrying markings in green felt-tip,
but always, where there are books
and a landing, managing to fit;

that marriage has lumps like
their button-backed sofa, constantly,
shortly, about to be stuffed;

and that love grows fat
as their squinting cat, swelling
round as a loaf from her basket.

I wish you years that shape, that form,
and a pond in a Sunday, urban garden;
where you'll see your joined reflection tremble,

stand and watch the waterboatmen
skate with ease across the surface tension.

Julia Copus

TOLGA BALOGLU

JULIA COPUS was born in 1969 in London. She went to Durham University and has since worked variously as a copywriter, a second-hand bookseller, a candlemaker, a teacher in Turkey, and a writer-in-residence in her home city of Southampton. Her poems view some of the most turbulent moments in life through a sharp, clear lens: mature, uncomfortably honest, uncompromising. She received an Eric Gregory Award in 1994. Her first book was a Poetry Book Society Recommendation, and was shortlisted for the Forward Prize for Best First Collection. ●

Selection from: *The Shuttered Eye* (1995 Bloodaxe).

Miss Havisham's Letter

Darling, there is nothing between us that cannot be
restored. So much remains of the good times: did I tell you

how, on the eve of our day, while in my under-garments,
I leaned forward and felt the full weight of my breasts

in my own hands! And such pleasures have been replaced
by other pleasures – a kind of wisdom: my eye knows

the very corner of my eye, and my mouth has learned
to use its various muscles to full effect –

When my girl comes with food I pull a perfect scowl,
but I do not refuse the tasteless sops she brings:

how else shall I sustain myself! Darling, the dress
outgrew me long ago. I hear it sometimes

cracking in its paper where the silkworms
shift and slide. It is trying to make a life for itself.

And my small night table is shaping an effigy
of you; it sags with all the candles I have burned.

Pray God that you will be here soon; the furniture
is weary, my darling, of the names I am forever

fingering into its dust.

Masaccio's *Expulsion from Paradise*

I *Eve*

With one thumb extended he could eclipse the whole
naked length of her. He began to think of her face
beneath it; the dampness of clay; how it would feel
to smooth her small features to hollows. He imagined

his thumb pushing into the darkness of her
gaping mouth (if you lean in close you'll hear
the gargled moans lodged deep in her throat)
and once he'd smudged her eyes shut it was clear

she wouldn't want to open them again.
Her face is a mask; her hands like the hands of Venus
in the Pisa Duoma, concealing the sin
of nipple and vulva: *Shame*, they are saying, *Shame*.

II *Adam*

Like a convict emerging from court to the angry
flash of paparazzi he shields himself. *At which moment,*
he demands, *was I the richer – then, when I was hungry,
or now, being full? O there is a deep deep hole*

inside me and a chill wind stirs. He curls
his shoulders, steels himself, turning inwards, in-
coiled for the voice of God is always at his back.
And the shadows of his ribs, his fallen chin

lie like stigmata on his skin. Above his head,
in a world of muted parchment-browns, the Angel's
blood-skirts go flaming, and he lifts a maledictory sword,
feeling the stretch of his wing, the muscled length of it.

*

Woman holds herself straight, forcing her hurt face skywards.
And Man walks blind beside her, surveys himself through
the vast dark of his hands. They move as one but
separately now. Not looking. Not touching. Not wanting to.

Pulling the Ivy

I

There was an avenue
of cedars all the way up

to the home where they
kept you because

your chest refused
to open itself out. It was

stubborn, they said, and you
looked up at me, grinning,

your small white face
all dimples, your bronchial

muscle clenched like a fist.
What I remember most

is the walls splashed
with primaries, bright

cartoon corridors that led
to your bed, and the smiles –

Mum, Dad and the nurses in the days
when we were all together still.

Or not quite apart. Outside
it was always Summer – rows

of lavender; I remember
the smell of it and its powder-soft

hue that would have come right
up over my head, except

I refused to stand next to it
to have my picture taken.

II

Dad got married yesterday.
At the ceremony

I wore ringlets, a green
ribbon and you helped

pull the ivy for my
bouquet, easing off

the tiny aerial rootlets,
one by one.

III

They joined hands, and through the image-
cluttered windows I saw the thick

velvet throats of the pasque-flowers
open for the sun: *all that I am*

I give to you. In the silence
they kept – which we all

kept – I heard you, for the first time,
breathing easily.

The Back Seat of My Mother's Car

We left before I had time
to comfort you, to tell you that we nearly touched
hands in that vacuous half-dark. I wanted
to stem the burning waters running over me like tiny
rivers down my face and legs, but at the same time I was reaching out
for the slit in the window where the sky streamed in,
cold as ether, and I could see your fat mole-fingers grasping
the dusty August air. I pressed my face to the glass;
I was calling to you – *Daddy!* – as we screeched away into
the distance, my own hand tingling like an amputation.
You were mouthing something I still remember, the noiseless words
piercing me like that catgut shriek that flew up, furious as a sunset
pouring itself out against the sky. The ensuing silence
was the one clear thing I could decipher –
the roar of the engine drowning your voice,
with the cool slick glass between us.

With the cool slick glass between us,
the roar of the engine drowning, your voice
was the one clear thing I could decipher –
pouring itself out against the sky, the ensuing silence
piercing me like that catgut shriek that flew up, furious as a sunset.
You were mouthing something: I still remember the noiseless words,
the distance, my own hand tingling like an amputation.
I was calling to you, Daddy, as we screeched away into
the dusty August air. I pressed my face to the glass,
cold as ether, and I could see your fat mole-fingers grasping
for the slit in the window where the sky streamed in
rivers down my face and legs, but at the same time I was reaching out
to stem the burning waters running over me like tiny
hands in that vacuous half-dark. I wanted
to comfort you, to tell you that we nearly touched.
We left before I had time.

Jane Duran

MARK GERSON

JANE DURAN was born in Cuba, brought up in the USA and in Chile, and has lived in England for the last thirty years. Her poems offer searing insights into the longing for and inability to have children, quirky memories of dancefloors, dreams and distant countries – all drawn with a true lyricism and a deft skill. She has been widely published in anthologies, journals and newspapers, and in 1995 she won the Forward Prize for Best First Collection. She lives and works in London. ●

Selection from: *Breathe Now, Breathe* (1995 Enitharmon).

The Mere Pleasure of Flying

This has happened before:
the unlikely loading of my carcass towards sky,
a redistribution of weight
pulling up just under my arms – lifting me
over low munching things,
a scarf through a ring.

The ship leaves its harbour on spidery feet
past pine trees etcetera at the end of the promontory
and unlikely, unlikely – alone in the air
I strengthen against the blue tonnage, the stopping

and sweep past the tree where all fruits jangle.
The grape the banana the mango the apple
detach from their stems and hang independently.

From end to end of me, over house masses – flotillas –
octagonal cinemas, glass dreadlocks of winter,
the sky feathery, layered, tumbles alongside me
not remote now. I fly

past the silent in twos, the speakers in threes
in the parks and the alleyways, on the docks and the gangways,
with two jets of water from dragon-fish nostrils –

an end of day celebration for things grounded and cornered,
all looking up, amazed and unworthy

to see me struggling in my element,
panting, held fast against the sky.

For the Woman Who Dressed Up
to Listen to Gigli on the Radio

On her evening off
she put on her green silk
dress loose at the waist
with tiny pleats flaring
at the wrists
and below the knee.
She tidied the sitting-room
right above the kitchen
and turned on the radio
to listen to Beniamino Gigli.

Downstairs the family
made do without her,
took the ham from the fridge,
shook out the tablecloth,
left the dishes in the sink.
There was no need
to do them. Outside the snow
was falling, the voice of
Gigli beginning.

The lamp unburdened
its light into the room.
Her manuscript of silk shone.
She did not understand
the Italian when Gigli sang
to her and her alone,
ah! completely alone with him.

Stillborn

This hurt has beat so long,
turns up with the tide
each month – memorial.

The midwife waits by the bed.
A hand rests on my belly,
trails its design
with sympathy.
Who weeps with me?
I do not recognise
the long white hair.

Bygone – the fire escape,
a point of entry,
a wedge.
The fire hand is austere
all night long
all labour long
undoing.

I touch your foot
before you go
stepping blindly off
no toehold, no notches
to catch at
nothing binding, nothing soft

our child
dropped down through time
through the slats
like a dime.

Here in my bed
I exchange coinage with the night.
The curtain whisks up – seagull edge,
its white barely flaring.
The roof is smitten with rain
and the ends of stories.

Mr Teller the Piano Teacher

He stood by the piano for an hour, every Wednesday
he took Amanda's plump fingers and pressed them on the keys.
Clumsy entrances: the notes dragged out their prey
from all corners of the house.

A mother opened the door to the kitchen to hear better.
She wore the same dress always, with blue roses
here and there. Tinkle, crash – the dishes and the piano.
A father hummed the tunes, lagging behind.

A sister with a wide belt too tight to breathe properly
and a stone digging into the nape of her neck, ran upstairs,
slammed the door of her bedroom. The arpeggios stumbled
round and round that house with closed windows.

After the lesson Mr Teller, knowing the secrets of the sonata,
sat down to play for a few moments, just a few,
to show Amanda what he could have been,
what she could be, one day.

Music of stairwells, music dripped from inkwells.
The notes were for him. Those Wednesday evenings
when he sat at the piano thinking of himself as he was
then, of his student room matted with night

and how he opened the casement
how the pointed roofs, the largeness of snow held him.

Time Zones

It will be cold now in Crete.
They will be pulling out
from the chests the locked-in
rugs. They will draw in
from the trees for needy
breakfasts. The sheep will blur.

It will be dark and never
dark in New York, this time.
Streets will speed by
with their ice lights
hurting. Bar doors
will be half open,
the rich light dropping its force
on the sidewalk
like the girl in a blue
leotard, collapsing to rest
on the dance studio floor.

In Bangladesh it will be afternoon
already. All the afternoons
that have ever been
will be in it, of it.
The entrances to villages
will be jugs
turned inside out –
smooth lemon walls,
pathways – the rub of ginger.

In Peru couples will be asleep
in the presence of mountains,
of heavy rivers.
Hardly a match will burn
in the Andes, the extinguishing
torrents.

Torrents will happen,
wind, ice.
In all these places we have been
there will be no trace of us.

Gillian Ferguson

GILLIAN FERGUSON was born in 1965. She studied Philosophy at Edinburgh University, tutored for the Open University and worked as a wildlife and botanical illustrator before moving to journalism. The intricacies of the natural world infuse her work, shedding light on the still more curious goings-on of the human sphere. Gillian Ferguson was awarded a Scottish Arts Council Writer's Bursary in 1993. She is the television critic for *Scotland on Sunday*. ●

SCOTLAND ON SUNDAY

Selection from: *Air for Sleeping Fish* (1997 Bloodaxe).

The Swimming Pool Ghost

In splintering shallows at the local pool,
a ghost shifts – a shoal of pink minnows
that never comes up for air again.

A terminal dive into three feet of thin water.
Corrugated spine. Skull grenade.

Climbing from the slow skin
of emptied indoor water,
a goggled woman scoured
her shocked body raw.

You can mistake him for the breathless lengths
of underwater swimmers, but pass clean through –
a touch of cold current as he disperses.

No mermaids here.
No scenic carcasses of sunken ships.
Nothing of how my friend saw his death
as he drowned in a beautiful place:
a Mexican bay in the evening
like a basin of blood.

Water slapped kisses on his lips,
a mute choir of fancy-coloured fish
mouthing in the waves –
lungs could breathe water
like the living sponge.

The swimming pool ghost
ripples around children –
churning cherubs with plastic wings –
because there was no time
to make tableaux of his death,
for mouths cushioning bedside air
with comfortable words.

Because he died in the wrong metaphor
like a baby dropped in a font.

Because sudden death is crime
against the spirit, he waits
at the scene for a just court.

When the pool is drained,
will he swim in air
like a wingless salmon,

or rush to the sluice –
to dive, be swallowed
by bottomless sea?

Slugs

Without the decency of shells,
slugs reveal themselves
on the steps suddenly lit.

Uniform brown,
the slow armourless army
advances in silent night manoeuvres.

Bodies seethe,
dumb but wounded
by light melting on the move.

A mucous map
smears the stones;
the route of some repulsive purpose –

but blind
they do not stumble,
one long belly

can go no lower;
all obstacles
patiently assailed.

Connoisseurs of air,
horns tremble
at exquisite samples –

the breath of flowers,
leaf-stir,
sun-burned soil.

The moon transfigures
slime – they bleed
original silver

as crude worms
spin silk.
Like a life trail

viscid with sin
polished
by God.

In Hospital-land

A virus nibbled the delicacy of my father's brain.
Nonsense streamed from his cracked lips,
hitching a ride on galloping grammar –

the kind in the book I feared so much
I weighted it nightly with my heaviest toys
in case the pictures squeezed out into my dreams –

a man-sized rabbit with red-jelly eyes
whose words jitter me still when late and wired,
and her, blonde and banded just like me

holding a baby which turned to a pig
as under my hands now you might turn to a corpse –
why was there no blood from such unusual violence?

The delicate curve of long flamingo necks
beating terrified hedgehog spikes –
a voice saying 'Off with his head' as the only solution.

I ran down a corridor horribly bright
as if my screams might call you back
from checking out rumours of irresistible light,

and when I was so small I looked at feet,
a hand held out a glass of water,
a gesture as plain as a label saying DRINK ME.

Why did she take the poisonous potion?
Why didn't she just shout DADDY
who would make it all stop?

Janet Fisher

CLAIRE McNAMEE

JANET FISHER was born in Birmingham in 1943 and grew up in the North Oxfordshire countryside. She studied law at Bristol University and later worked in publishing until her sons were born. Her poems illuminate small moments between people, passing threads of conversation, and make of them something resonant and universal. Janet Fisher lives in Huddersfield where she is co-director (with Peter Sansom) of The Poetry Business. ●

Selection from: *Listening to Dancing* (1996 Smith/Doorstop).

A Life

He forced his way into it, a near shave.
The strawberry mark on his neck, the thick tongue:
the midwife gave thumbs down as she left by the back gate
to Mrs B next door peering behind curtains.
They're past it, must have been an old packet,
she muttered, wheeling her bike down the side.

He didn't walk till three. Once, stood at the bath side
he ate a bar of soap and half a tube of Colgate
while his father was having a shit and a shave,
blew minty bubbles through the open end of the packet
and his dad thought he was fitting, shoved a flannel over his tongue,
parcelled his body tight in the shower curtains,

cut his foot on his razor, now knowing for certain
the lad would be always on the outside,
always last to be picked for the team; and his tongue
stuck to his mouth. He called him a young shaver.
washed him, belted him tight to the safety gate,
warned his mother mustn't know or they'd both catch a packet.

They scraped and saved for private school, but had to pack it
in. Was it his refusal to work, keep clean, shave,
or his knowledge of markets and his small deals on the side?
Denied escape, he gave them the rough edge of his tongue,
spent his teens in his room screaming, climbing the curtains.
He plotted possibilities, routes to the other side of the gate.

At 18 he cut and ran to a basement in Margate.
Its separate entrance was worth a packet;
though the mould glowed in the dark he didn't need curtains.
He built up his contacts, got rich, even put a bit aside.
Each night in his white trilby, a splash of aftershave,
a little something dissolved on the back of the tongue,

he would wink at himself in the mirror, his tongue
flicking his lips like a cat's, slip behind curtains
at the back of cafés, dispensing his small packets
like a teacher with pencils, closing the floodgate
on conscience. He fixed it himself, cutting down the side
with a clear eye, a sharp blade, a clean shave.

Caught, strip searched, head shaved, in a room without curtains.
names, dates, on the tip of his tongue. Then they slammed the gate.
And two people grieved a packet, the rest put it to one side.

Gooseflesh

She even meditates on rites of passage,
decides to celebrate, invite the village.
This is the last one before the big one.
Her body has kept up with fashion:
from sixties pill to menopause,
it's all on the women's page of course.
Her swinging belt is notched with stars.

Some things are not on her agenda
but what *did* she want: a wife, a plumber,
cards on the table and cake for breakfast.
Head rules heart and she'll leave feet first,
the last chocolate in the box.
The earth has opened up its plot.
She grows funny plants from the seeds
her son gave her. Calls them weeds.
The face in the bathroom mirror stinks
of character. As she dyes her hair in the sink,
the red stains lurking round the spout
tell her this time they won't wash out.

Camp

If you do not have a towel
you will be punished.
You clench it in your knees when you wash.
If you put it down it will vanish.
If you do not wash you will be punished.

You carry your hunger everywhere.
a dead animal on your back.
You cannot put it down
not even for a second.

'There are only so many words'

There are only so many words
and I'm stuck with the ones I've got:
lines drawn desperately between roads,
the singing trees, their lost leaves,
rats running from the blaze.

'Dad died yesterday, last week, last year.'
The echoes grow fainter,
footsteps down a corridor.
swing doors and the smell of dinners,
a notice by a phone: if you are lost, ring here.

It's February But

fog and thaw make the garden smell like Christmas.
Crouched on a low chair at midnight, I'm shifting
bills and statements in search of investments
and debtors. There are none. What's here is here:
enough in the bank for a decent cremation,
no flowers, and an empty cottage
we visit tomorrow to clear of novels
and spoons, suits by now holding the shape
of the hangers, shoes well polished, treed,
unworn. Photos and letters were collected
weeks back, to be done something with.

Then, though I've been through it
a dozen times, under some carbons stashed
at the bottom of the file box: an envelope of papers.
Time has slit their creases like a knife; I lay out
the pieces. They're not, as you'd think,
twelve and a half per cent Treasury Stock redeemable
any day now, but their birth certificates: hers, West Ham
nineteen fourteen, mother Edith, father Samuel,
journeyman tool maker; his, Mandalay, nineteen-
o-two, illegible not by age but its unknown script,
curly like Celtic runes, and no signature I can make out.

Pearls

The Archangel bears down from his pinnacle,
his flaming sword ravaging the pagan,
the tourist, sellers of novelty monks
and snow scenes of Mont St Michel.

Seven evenings watching sunsets beyond the islands:
the chrysanthemum, the coughdrop, the candyfloss,
the red hot poker, three blank looks.

By Tuesday we yearn for interiors, forests,
anything unconnected with the sea.
We lunch in the garden, the cherry tree
heavy with unformed fruit. The lawn
sprouts mushrooms, but we do not trust them.

A hot afternoon outside the café, oysters in boxes,
cheap. They would slip down so easily.
My stomach tightens: the price is too high.

Soaping a flannel I count seven reasons for owning a bidet:
before after after during when right foot left foot.

The bikers get up another chorus of 'Eye of the Tiger'
as France backs off, richer for having met us.

Linda France

RUFUS FRANCE

Selection from: *Red* (1992), *The Gentleness of the Very Tall* (1994), *Storyville* (1997): all Bloodaxe.

LINDA FRANCE was born in Newcastle in 1958. After living in Dorset, Leeds, London and Amsterdam, she returned to the North East in 1981 to live in Northumberland. Her poems are wide-ranging, richly-textured, bold and sensuous. Her second collection was a Poetry Book Society Recommendation, and she was awarded the Arts Foundation's first Poetry Fellowship in 1993. Her anthology for Bloodaxe, *Sixty Women Poets* (1993), was a landmark. A freelance writer, she has worked on several collaborations with artists. She has two children. ●

Mess With It

> *'If you don't know what jazz is, don't mess with it.'*
> FATS WALLER

It creeps up behind you on all fours,
a reed between its teeth, so quiet
you barely notice. Until it's too late:
smoky breath tickles your neck keening
its sweetness and you toss back your head
in red surrender. The blood beneath your skin
runs hot as sex, cold as death. You borrow
its velvet pelt, watching your face lost
in the mirror of its Spanish eyes.
If you have to ask what it is,
you'll probably never know.

It's a secret for anyone with ears,
an inkling to dance like an oyster
with a black pearl heart. The sea
isn't deep enough for its blue.
It swims you till your lips are salt
and crazy. Never was an ache more
beautiful; like the love you fall into
too easy. If you don't know what it is,
don't mess with it.

It will score your belly with gorgeous claws,
tug your guts into tight cords.
You'll lose yourself in its glorious bite
and no one will believe the height
of your eyes. It will love you then leave you
with just a brush of silver on the rim
of your high-hat. And when the sun goes down
you'll catch yourself swaying to the fragrance
of sweating lilies, blowing their white horns
as if there was no tomorrow.
There isn't. You know what it is.
Love it while it lasts. Mess with it.

...What I Know Now
(FROM *On the Game*)

Now I know they're all the same. A standing cock
has no conscience: punter, lover or pimp.

Now I know I was just kidding myself;
couldn't see the gold in his eyes
was my own light. Even after that night
he broke me in with a gang of his mates:
I should have run but I could hardly walk.
He said sorry, standing in my blind spot.

Now I know the way to a man's heart
is through his pocket. All there was left of me
were the bruises, the scars his knife etched
in my skin: his brand, our secret binding.
I looked in the mirror and saw a whore
waiting to be transformed into a dream princess.

Now I know the only way to get out
of it is to get out of it. But what's
crooked can never be straight. He's doing time
for setting a girl on fire. *Big Car Small Dick.*
He didn't laugh. That could have been me,
burnt like so much waste paper.

Now I know I'll never do it again
for anyone else. I am the star of my own story.
Cocaine's my ponce. That's all that gets me up
and on the streets. The twitches, the shakes, they don't
go away but I'm not in the business
of kidding myself, not any more. Not now I know.

The Gentleness of the Very Tall
(after Chagall's 'La Maison Rouge')

Even the tallest didn't remember
Napoleon saying *Let them eat leaves.*
Each bite of apricot moon teased hunger,

buttery and forgetful, a dark stone
for a heart gritting its little white pip
of heaven. Despite their facility
for sleight and coaxing, hands just can't manage

pollination by air. One finger might
journey the curve of a thigh or a scythe,
the white of one eye. Or two. Isn't
any the wiser, though soothed by simply

moving, at least the possibility
of gentleness. Why else feel air thinning
with altitude, with the brassy sound

of a very beautiful musical
instrument, what happens to heat when
silence rises. And never ends. Even
when the tallest must climb up trees to see

the sun and the moon shine together
in the sky over red rooftops, quite
a small woman breathing mists on a mirror,
seeding oceans: storms, tranquillity, nectar.

Meteorology

Afterwards she blamed it on the wind, cold
in the air like someone's breath in her ear.
And listening was the mistake she made,
wishing its wild stories were really true.
The almanac they consulted lied,
its wicked lips closing and opening,
an oracle of storms, mercury trapped
in blue glass. And afterwards that something
had happened, something beginning with *m*,
was all she knew, that tasted like the wind,
smoke and citrus, someone else's perfume.
The weather changed: something lost, something gained,
the rain, filled the space between them, so far
apart, buckets and buckets of weather.

New York Spring

He had the nerve to say *Let's be grown-up about this.*
Like hell. And him acting like a kid who wants jello
with his Häagen-Dazs. Let him eat grown-up pussy.
With claws. I left as sharp as my little beauties.
All that stylish white we worked our asses off for
didn't look so clean after he told me what he told me
was all. Stupid, trying to deny a crop of blonde hairs
marbling the sheets when we're both shades of New England brown.
His downfall: never learning to use the washing-machine.

When a mutual friend let slip they'd gone away for a time,
I didn't even need to think; still kept the key
to the loft on my fob. Let myself in like a regular burglar,
come to claim something I couldn't take home in a bag
marked swag; but just as desirable. And it was as if I'd grown-up,
died a little and nothing I touched would ever be the same.
I exchanged greetings with the washing-machine,
borrowed its black snake of a hose and soaked the whole place
in high-pressure tears. All the things we'd bought together

and loved, I purified with water, an act of defiant surrender.
Good and wet, I sprinkled it thick with seeds
from the wholefood store, mustard and cress, 100% organic.
Millions of little dots, beige and ochre, an experiment
after Lichtenstein. Then I turned the heating on high,
shut the door up tight. The saddest thing is, I can only imagine
their faces when they opened the door, expecting
soothing sterile white, to find a ripening anarchy of green,
their very own pastoral symphony, its pungent smell addling the air:

my parting gift, a blessing grown despite neglect,
just a little something they'd never forget,
the colour of an old friend's eyes.

Chip City

The train that carried me there was a chip,
crunching along tracks made of chips.
When I got off, the streets were paved with chips,
crisp and golden. There were vertical chips
for street-lights, sprinkling a salty glow at night
when newspapers flew in the spaces between chips
and roosted, rustling their greasy wings.
The people were chips with clothes on,
pushing chips on wheels, walking chips on leads,
chips that cried and barked. They knew they were all chips
off the old block and they'd never drive turbo chips,
never live in semi-detached chips;
they'd never have a body like a french fry
however hard they tried to make the fat fly.
And for this they all had chips
on their shoulders, soused in vinegar.
And why not when there was nothing but chips,
wrapped or open, the only word on everyone's lips,
larding the city's wriggling hips,
drifting out to sea like the ghost of fish and ships?

The Eater of Wives

Call me old-fashioned, but I'm never mean
with saffron. How many times have I heard
my own grandmother say the man who's tired
of good food, cooked with love, is a man dying?

Mornings, it's true, I'm moody and blinking
before I dress my eyes with the fragrant scales
of fish. I gave up meat years ago. God knows,

it's taken me forty years to feel this
restless, spicing my hollow nights with women
who taste like apples, cherries, pears. I eat out
in every town. And the little lady
at home feeds me her pretzel arms, her marzipan arse.

I hate sleeping in the shell of my own breath
so I follow the raw scent of my sweat,

what's cooking between their legs; suck them dry
as cocktail martinis till my head spins
with their names. *Charlotte. Rosemary. Hélène.*

I just pick up the phone; hear my voice saying
Remember me? bubbling like a thick soup
of oysters and mussels from the Bay
of Angels. Listen, all I want is the best, some
girl who'll eat me back, lick the plate clean.

Elizabeth Garrett

ELIZABETH GARRETT was born in 1958 in London. She grew up in the Channel Islands and studied at Oxford University. Her poetry displays a formal grace and sinewy intelligence across subjects as diverse as a bowl of porridge, a sculpture by Degas or the eternal themes of love, memory, family and time. Her collection *The Rule of Three* was selected for the New Generation poetry promotion in 1994. Elizabeth Garrett lives and works in Oxford. ●

ALISON RICHARDS

Selection from: *The Rule of Three* (1991 Bloodaxe), *A Two-Part Invention* (1998 Bloodaxe).

Love's Parallel

Since, in the loop of time this will return
To where it began – the poem unwritten
And the heartland squared and folded
On itself – know that last night I followed

A thought of you to the sheer face of love,
My only bearings the imperative of
Displacement, here, in a foreign bed,
Your absent body plotting a curve

Against mine. Something about the cold
Flank of the hill I lay below, curled
Like a fossil, resisted the mind's compass,
Halting here, dark as despair's impasse

Till dawn. Till this – this alchemy of frost
Defining the hill's entire circumference,
So, from the summit, what the map withheld
Of magnitude lies suddenly revealed:

For distance is our love's cool parallel,
And ours the chaste harmony of this hill's
Contours – that neither break, nor touch, but hold
The heart's sheer gradient, encircled.

History Goes to Work

The soft-boiled egg is emptied
But makes a humpty-dumpty head
Reversed. Numbskull! Bald pate!
You know the spoon's importunate
Knock knock will wake the dead.

The silver spoon lies on its back
And spoons the room all up-
Side-down but never spills a drop:
The ovoid walls adapt their laws
And never show a crack.

The egg lies in the silver spoon
And yolkless words lie on the tongue
And all that's in the spoon-shaped room
Swears it is square; no books
Were cooked. The egg is done.

Remorse rests in its velvet drawer
Lapped in the sleep of metaphor,
The soul rests in the open palm
And will not put its shell back on,
And calmly waits for more.

The Womanhood

It was the colour of incense
And it drove men wild.
She wore it like the wind
And the devil smiled
To see such innocence
In a grown-up child.

Subtleties she practised
Till they had her by heart –
Played her like the psaltery
So no man could part
Her fingers' lattice
From their naked art.

It was the flame's syllable
And the ferryman's fee.
She sung men to heaven
Where she turned them free
With the taste of obol
Where her name should be.

Lost Property

Kneel, and let us pray for the departed:
A sulphurous incense chokes the station vaults,
A pigeon coughs; the platform is deserted.
Guilty-eyed, while others slept in prayer
I scoured the hassock's cross-stitch for some fault
As though it were my soul; and found none there.

A labour of devotion: pious kisses
Smothering the cushion where my knees
Grew numb and bore the imprint of those stitches.
Burden of the Cross. A priest intones,
Feet shuffle for Communion to ease
The weight, and catch the last train home.

The rails are silent, empty as the aisle
When rush-hour's past. A platform sweeper brushes
Up confetti into piles.
It's growing dark. A thin girl stands and watches
As he sweeps the crumbs that drowsy birds
Have missed. I wake. And there are words
For this; but none so fittingly expressed
As by my own hand cupped around my breast.

Mimesis

Dragged, drenched, from sleep, by horror
Of smothering, I found your hot
Wet head too close to my heart.

Mortified by neglect following so hard
On your first breath, I cradled
Your head back to its own bed,

My fingers trembling while the swell
Of darkness stilled in the darker well
Of all wishing – your fontanelle;

Only to find you there, absolute and apart
In unrippled sleep, no more a part
Of me than this mockery of the art

Of mothering: my own breast taut
With a need in these hands so hot
It wept milk straight from my chilled heart.

Airborne

Upupup! The light percussive
Of your lips, a chick's nib
Tapping in the shell – the womb!
The cell! your gaze like water
Questing at the window's sill;
Well, I will let it spill right over
Till it floods the whole window
And your face hangs luminous
As Betelgeuse in heaven. So
I would have the glass hold you for ever.

And as I lift, cropping your blonde
Head, the moon swings its sickle.
Silence. Then your low *mooaan*
Burdening the world – as if that blade
Had reaped the fullness of all pain.
Each day you grow further from home, blazing
Your trail through the tongue's galaxy,
And either my arms deceive me, or
The hour the dark tide cast you speechless
On my shore, you did weigh more.

Moules à la Marinière

We scoured the secret places of the creek,
Parting blistered fronds of bladder-wrack
To find the concupiscent clusters, rocked
In their granite crèche. Jack-knives prised
The molluscs out. Slick blue-blacks bruised
Slowly dull; and the sea expunged our tracks.

Bouquet of Muscadet, bouquet garni recall
The tuck and chuckle of mussels in a bucket
Behind the door. Damp and aromatic,
Steam insinuates itself into all
The kitchen clefts, and clings in briny beads
Above the flame where mussels chirp and wheeze.

I pour on wine; it seems they beg for more,
The beaked shells yearning wide as if in song –
Yet dumb – and lewdly lolling parrot-tongues.
Cream licks the back of a spoon and drawls a slur
Of unctuous benediction for this feast.
We smooth our cassocks; bow our heads; and eat.

It rained all night as though to wash away
A brininess that tanged the atmosphere:
Dreams – of forbidden fruit, of *fruits de mer*
Wrenched from their secret beds, of tastes that lay
Like sea's after-sting on the tongue. Still lingers
A trace of guilt. I wash my salty fingers.

Lavinia Greenlaw

MARK CHICHESTER-CLARK

Selection from: *Night Photo-graph* (1993 Faber), *A World Where News Travelled Slowly* (1997 Faber)

LAVINIA GREENLAW was born in 1962 in London, where she still lives. She worked in publishing, as part of the literature team at the South Bank Centre and as Literature Officer for London Arts Board before turning freelance. Fascinated by both science and history, her poetry interweaves an intelligent, subtle combination of the personal, the bizarre, the everyday and the remarkable. She won an Eric Gregory Award in 1990, and was selected for the New Generation promotion in 1994. In 1995 she received an Arts Council of England Writer's Award and was writer in residence at the Science Museum and a fellow at Amherst College, Massachusetts. ●

A World Where News Travelled Slowly

It could take from Monday to Thursday
and three horses. The ink was unstable,
the characters cramped, the paper tore where it creased.
Stained with the leather and sweat of its journey,
the envelope absorbed each climatic shift,
as well as the salt and grease of the rider
who handed it over with a four-day chance
that by now things were different and while the head
had to listen, the heart could wait.

Semaphore was invented at a time of revolution;
the judgement of swing in a vertical arm.
News travelled letter by letter, along a chain of towers,
each built within telescopic distance of the next.
The clattering mechanics of the six-shutter telegraph
still took three men with all their variables
added to those of light and weather,
to read, record and pass the message on.

Now words are faster, smaller, harder
... we're almost talking in one another's arms.
Coded and squeezed, what chance has my voice
to reach your voice unaltered and then to leave no trace?

Nets tighten across the sky and the sea bed.
When London made contact with New York,
there were such fireworks, City Hall caught light.
It could have burned to the ground.

Boris Goes Fishing
(for Bill Swainson)

In my classroom Russia you commented on the weather,
said goodbye to Mother and goodbye to Father,
while I struggled with the tenses
that would let you spend the day by the lake.
Your journey was uneventful. You did not
get lost in a forest, follow strange music
and wander off a path that never saw daylight
to be seduced by a snow queen and rescued by wolves.
I couldn't even send you to Samarkand
to save a princess from being boiled in oil.

You were allowed a blue sky and a friendly dog,
when what you really wanted was a tidal wave
that would empty the Baltic into your basket.
The day passed quietly. You caught three fish
and I managed to get the dog to fall into the water.
At home that evening, Father commented on the weather
while Mother cooked the fish. They could have been
sturgeon travelled north from the Caspian Sea,
pregnant with caviar, flavoured with bison's grass
and served in a blaze of vodka, but I did not

go into detail. Boris, you were a nice boy,
but my hand was more used to carving a desk
than filling a notebook with cramped Cyrillics.
I was fourteen and knew the Russia of storybooks;
I didn't want to make space for the wild grammar,
soft adjectives, accusatives and instrumentals
that would take you there. Instead, you went
to bed at eight o'clock. Mother tucked you up and
commented on the weather. I could not pronounce 'revolution',
so I shut you in a drawer and went dancing.

The Earliest Known Representation of a Storm in Western Art

Like an accident or an insistence, without model or precedent,
water was rising and water would fall and flatten a picture
strung out on perspective with over-muscled jumpy horses,
men about to kneel, about to ride. The envoy whose story it was
suffered from dust, charm and the wary illumination

of bulbs that drooped from tendrils of wiring, light metered
by collection boxes, the cathedral's erratic pulse. I chose
a child saint who walked among victims of the plague
in a besieged city and died young. I rehearsed her name
but on that cold hard day the sky kept its distance.

I come home and the street is a river, the roof is flotsam,
chimneys are periscopes, gutters fountain, pavements lagoon.
It has rained for so long that we should have faith in it, faith
in the sea and the boat and the horses. Give me your hand,
love, look down, we are flying over our lives.

Millefiori
(for Don Paterson)

He preferred his glass eye to be of itself,
vitreous not ocular
or even optically convincing.

Without pupil or iris, allowed to risk
its stubbornly fluid nature,
the blue held everything.

It liquefied candlelight
and clouded over in winter.
Once, at the opera, an aria

built wave upon wave of sound,
higher and closer till it struck
the resonant frequency

of blue glass
and the molecules of his eye
oscillated into a thousand flowers.

Five O'Clock Opera

This cavernous apartment is ours on four months' good will,
like the industrial washing-machine and pocket transistor:
our two kinds of noise. What else? My mother's letters
to my daughter, a subscription to delayed world news;
and a campaign of love-hate mail, broken-hearted
socialist realism, agony and baby talk.

The local radio station is on a sponsorship drive.
They raise the stakes each hour, as desolate and righteous
as their featured diva who is climbing ever higher
in the mountains, her echo fitfully insistent
on the last word. The clocks have already gone back.
Our afternoon gets caught in the dark.

Love from a Foreign City

Dearest, the cockroaches are having babies.
One fell from the ceiling into my gin
with no ill effects. Mother has been.
I showed her the bitemarks on the cot
and she gave me the name of her rat-catcher.
He was so impressed by the hole in her u-bend,
he took it home for his personal museum.

I cannot sleep. They are digging up children
on Hackney Marshes. The papers say
when that girl tried to scream for help,
the man cut her tongue out. Not far from here.
There have been more firebombs,
but only at dawn and out in the suburbs.
And a mortar attack. We heard it from the flat,
a thud like someone dropping a table.
They say the pond life coming out of the taps
is completely harmless. A law has been passed
on dangerous dogs: muzzles, tattoos, castration.
When the labrador over the road jumped up
to say hello to Billie, he wet himself.
The shops in North End Road are all closing.
You can't get your shoes mended anywhere.
The one-way system keeps changing direction,
I get lost a hundred yards from home.
There are parts of the new *A to Z* marked simply
'under development'. Even street names
have been demolished. There is typhoid in Finchley.
Mother has brought me a lavender tree.

Iron Lung

The ventriloquist's breath;
watch, while my lungs compress
it is the concertina pump that sighs.

Not a glass coffin, more obscure,
a dark room I cannot go into
but am locked into from the neck.

The pressure:
your hand on the small of my back,
a whispered imperative, I rise and fall.

The recovery of tension, I dream of it –
through a window, adjacent trains in a station,
how one must be moving if the other is still.

The Shape of Things

There is no eighty-eighth storey
from which to point out three buildings,
each the tallest in its time. I sleep but can't sleep

on the fourth floor of a deluded hotel.
In such an early industrial city,
this is as high, as late as it gets.

I have seen no one, heard only
the sigh of the exoskeletal lift,
the firedoors' groan and cough.

The trill of the Bakelite phone by my bed
I imagine, but not the two ballrooms,
theatrical staircase and slipping lock.

Someone has left a shadow on the carpet
as if, blinded by champagne and erotic waltzes,
they had made a grand unsteady staircase exit

and come to rest with their ear to the ground.
I lie, curl into it, hand on their hand,
neither wanting to be there nor to miss a beat.

The street-cleaning truck scrapes past.
Indecisive, I bring it back
again and again to straighten and empty

my dreams, body heat, talk of political death.
I grasp the receiver when the alarm call comes,
whisper *thank you, thank you...*

New Year's Eve

This city's architecture is characterised by the colonnades
under which we duck to avoid water bombs. In the square,
a wobbly guitar solo clogged with fuzz leads us to Beppe
whom, ten years earlier, you passed each Sunday
on the cathedral steps, perched on a Harley, just a g-string
in all weathers. Now he is clothed and sells cassettes.

Tonight's celebrations will be broadcast nationwide.
The TV crew erect their twenty-foot friendly animal logo.
In an alley, dancers struggle to dress: three doves, a crow,
dark and hooded... We guess the plot and move on.
Midnight finds us eating in a wood-panelled restaurant
where women hang fur coats on hooks by their chairs.

The men, like you, have beautiful skin. One tired child
grips a silver evening bag against her silver mohair top.
I have never seen you so drunk, so quizzical or so intent.
You push your tongue against my teeth and issue a warning.
As we leave, a waiter hands me flowers and laughs.
Silent, elated by cold air, we are drawn to each other

then drawn back, by what sounds like an executioner's drum,
to the square, now paved with broken glass and empty
but for crowd-control barriers and a few impromptu fires.
The police lean dreamily against their cars. We wander off
so you can call your oldest friend. I burn in my sleep.
We send no postcards, take no pictures.

Vona Groarke

VONA GROARKE was born in Edgeworthstown, Co. Longford and grew up on a farm near Athlone. She went to university in Dublin and Cork and later worked in the USA, the UK and Norway. These are brave, musical poems of the insides and outsides of buildings, the insides and outsides of people, and where in all of that we might find a sense of home. She has received the *Sunday Tribune* New Irish Writer of the Year Award and the Hennessy Cognac Award for Poetry. She divides her time between Dundalk, where she lives with her family, and Galway, where she is the current Writer-in-Residence at UCG. ●

Selection from: *Shale* (1994 Gallery Press).

Shale

What leaves us trembling in an empty house
is not the moon, my moon-eyed lover.
Say instead there was no moon
though for nine nights we stood

on the brow of the hill at midnight
and saw nothing that was not
contained in darkness, in the pier light,
our hands, and our lost house.

Small wonder that we tired of this
and chose instead to follow the road
to the back of the island, and broke
into the lighthouse-keeper's house.

We found the lower windows boarded up
and the doors held fast, but one.
Inside, we followed the drag of light
through empty rooms of magenta and sky blue.

This house has been decided by the sea.
These rooms are stones washed over by waves
and spray from the lighthouse
by which we undress

to kneel under the skylight.
Our hands and lips are smeared with blackberries.
Your skin, my sloe-skinned lover,
never so sweet, your hand so quiet.

The sea is breaking and unbreaking on the pier.
You and I are making love
in the lighthouse-keeper's house,
my moon-eyed, dark-eyed, fire-eyed lover.

What leaves us trembling in an empty room
is not the swell of darkness in our hands,
or the necklace of shale I made for you
that has grown warm between us.

Trousseau

I do not wear white as a general rule,
but that day in Finse, between trains,
I could have found a use
for even the veil and wedding-dress
I hadn't bothered with the day before.

While he was gone to check the times
I went through our holiday bags,
tossed our clothes onto the platform,
and picked out what was white, or almost white:
underwear mostly; socks; my slip; his torn T-shirt.

With these he helped me plot a line
laying each one down to touch another
so that they spanned from the tracks
to the unpacked snow
behind the station-house.

When our train pulled out again
we were bickering over the window seat
from which we could just about make out
a broken trail of underwear
subsiding in the snow.

Not even the final blaze of ice
seen from the westbound Oslo train
was as lavish, as immediate as this:
our wedding gift to a world
that wanted nothing, held nothing of us.

The Riverbed

There is sun in the mirror, my head in the trees.
There is sun in the mirror without me.
I am lying face up on the riverbed.
My lover is swimming above me.

The ribbons he tied in my hair are gone,
gone back to their net in the water.
Instead I have silverweed, speedwell and rue,
where once I had his hands to lie on.

Instead I have silverweed, speedwell and rue,
where once I had his arms beneath me.
His body may come as his body has gone –
and the marl will close over again.

Where are your silverweed, your speedwell now?
They have all gone under the water.
Where is your face in the river now?
Drifting upstream to the moon.

I have walked on the floor of the river with you
I have walked on the floor of the river.
I would lie on the bed of the river with you.
I will lie on the bed of the river.

The History of My Father's House

Was that the year the water froze
in the jug on the kitchen sink? Or was that
the year the wind took the back barn door?
You said it was found a townland away,

not a scratch on it, just lost.
I am trying to find out the year this house –
my father's house – was built.
You are remembering not by year,

but by keepsake and event.
You tell me there is a photograph
of him in the pram on the avenue.
But this house has no avenue

and is only as old as you decide it to be.
There have been years lived here:
storms, foxes, an argument over land,
a bracelet that he gave to you one night.

It is late. The story is an old one.
You tell me this: that you want me to know
you have a memory of your mother
when she answered your questions too.

That, even now, after all these years,
what you remember is how she
was standing close by the window,
concerned about the lateness of the hour.

Her hand lets fall the curtain.
She lights the lamp and wonders
if the fire will keep in until they come.
With all this, your questions are a nuisance.

You know, but continue, because
her answers (spare and to the point)
keep off the dark and remind her
that you are and will be there.

The Family Photograph

In the window of the drawing-room
there is a rush of white as you pass
in which the figure of your husband is,
for a moment, framed. He is watching you.

His father will come, of course,
and, although you had not planned it,
his beard will offset your lace dress,
and always it will seem that you were friends.

All morning, you had prepared the house
and now you have stepped out
to make sure that everything
is in its proper place: the railings whitened,

fresh gravel on the avenue, the glasshouse
crystal when you stand in the courtyard
expecting the carriage to arrive at any moment.
You are pleased with the day, all month it has been warm.

They say it will be one of the hottest summers
the world has ever known.
Today, your son is one year old.
Later, you will try to recall

how he felt in your arms –
the weight of him, the way he turned to you from sleep,
the exact moment when you knew he would cry
and the photograph be lost.

But it is not lost.
You stand, a well-appointed group
with an air of being pleasantly surprised.
You will come to love this photograph

and will remember how, when he had finished,
you invited the photographer inside
and how, in celebration of the day,
you drank a toast to him, and summer-time.

Sophie Hannah

SOPHIE HANNAH was born in Manchester in 1971. She studied English Literature and Spanish at the University there and still lives in the city, where she is Writer-in-Residence at the Portico Library. Her poems move between satire and tenderness with deft skill and wittily subversive use of traditional forms. In 1995 she received an Eric Gregory Award. ●

Selection from: *The Hero and the Girl Next Door* (1995 Carcanet), *Hotels like Houses* (1996 Carcanet).

Where is Talcott Parsons Now?

(Talcott Parsons was an American sociologist)

Could a man in your position
Ever love a girl like me?
Would you have to get permission
From the aristocracy?
Just a normal girl, no dowry,
With a house which, at first glance,
Looks like something drawn by Lowry?
Would we ever stand a chance?

Am I utterly deluded
Or could such a love exist?
Would I have to be included
In the Civil Honours List,
Hang about with landed gentry,
Or would access be denied?
Would there be a firm no entry
To all persons from Moss Side?

Are your exes all princesses
Who could spot a pea with ease?
Do they wear designer dresses
And have dinner with MPs?
Are they many times my betters
With their titles, wealth and fame?
Does each one of them have letters
Queueing up beside her name?

Would it be too much to handle?
Would your folks rewrite their wills?
Would it lead, perhaps, to scandal
Or some parliamentary bills?
Would the penalties be hefty?
Will we know until we've tried?
Is the heart a closet lefty
That will not be stratified?

I remember how I hated
Sociology at school
And I've only ever dated
Normal people as a rule.
Masses loving other masses
Maybe never need to learn
That ye olde social class is
Still a relevant concern.

Can mobility be hurried?
Where is Talcott Parsons now
When I need him, when I'm worried?
Do the text books not allow
For a man in your position
Just to have the briefest whirl
(In the Mills & Boon tradition)
With an ordinary girl?

Postcard from a Travel Snob

I do not wish that anyone were here.
This place is not a holiday resort
with karaoke nights and pints of beer
for drunken tourist types – perish the thought.

This is a peaceful place, untouched by man –
not like your seaside-town-consumer-hell.
I'm sleeping in a local farmer's van –
it's great. There's not a guest house or hotel

within a hundred miles. Nobody speaks
English (apart from me and rest assured,
I'm not your sun-and-sangria-two-weeks
small-minded-package-philistine-abroad).

When you're as multi-cultural as me,
your friends become wine connoisseurs, not drunks.
I'm not a British tourist in the sea;
I am an anthropologist in trunks.

The End of Love

The end of love should be a big event.
It should involve the hiring of a hall.
Why the hell not? It happens to us all.
Why should it pass without acknowledgement?

Suits should be dry-cleaned, invitations sent.
Whatever form it takes – a tiff, a brawl –
The end of love should be a big event.
It should involve the hiring of a hall.

Better than the unquestioning descent
Into the trap of silence, than the crawl
From visible to hidden, door to wall.

Get the announcements made, the money spent.
The end of love should be a big event.
It should involve the hiring of a hall.

Your Street Again

'Guess who I saw last night?' was all she said.
That, and the answer (you), was all it took,
And now I'm leafing through my *A-Z*
To find your street again. I had to look

Four years ago, and memorise the way:
Palatine, Central, Burton - halfway there.
I don't intend to visit you today
As I did then, and so I shouldn't care

Which road comes after which and where they lead.
I do, though. I repeat them name by name.
My house is here and yours is there. I need
To prove the space between them stays the same.

Symptoms

Although you have given me a stomach upset,
weak knees, a lurching heart, a fuzzy brain,
a high-pitched laugh, a monumental phone bill,
a feeling of unworthiness, sharp pain
when you are somewhere else, a guilty conscience,
a longing, and a dread of what's in store,
a pulse rate for the *Guinness Book of Records* –
life now is better than it was before.

Although you have given me a raging temper,
insomnia, a rising sense of panic,
a hopeless challenge, bouts of introspection,
raw, bitten nails, a voice that's strangely manic,
a selfish streak, a fear of isolation,
a silly smile, lips that are chapped and sore,
a running joke, a risk, an inspiration –
life now is better than it was before.

Although you have given me a premonition,
chattering teeth, a goal, a lot to lose,
a granted wish, mixed motives, superstitions,
hang-ups and headaches, fear of awful news,
a bubble in my throat, a dare to swallow,
a crack of light under a closing door,
the crude, fantastic prospect of forever –
life now is better than it was before.

Maggie Hannan

MOIRA CONWAY

MAGGIE HANNAN was born in 1962 in Wiltshire, and lived in Derbyshire, Cumbria and Hull before moving to Newcastle, where she has been Writer-in-Residence on the Internet, working from the University of Northumbria. Her poetry grips language itself, making it both subject and object of many of her poems. She is inventive, playful and knowing: the poems glitter with an intelligent dark humour. Maggie Hannan's *Liar, Jones* was shortlisted for the Forward Prize for Best First Collection. ●

Selection from: *Liar, Jones*
(1995 Bloodaxe).

Making Conversation

1 *Gesture*

Queer the way
the mouth let slip

the whether
or not of how

it might begin.
Rum the pantomime

of lips, the labial
shrug through which

the unspeakable
air was forced. Odd

the glottal break
kicking the throat

and busy the hands
and turned the back.

Queer the noise
and queer the pitch.

2 *Bow Wow*

The pitch not
of a lark, more

like bull – a bubble
of it, bellow. Below

the normal scale
but rising after

nap, cat nap.
Actually, barking.

Baulked at more
than merely

mewling, moaning –
oh dear, this

time groaning,
horsing, aping

all the zoo, and
tired. Dog-tired.

3 *Yo He Ho*

Dog-tired from this
huf puf seith that

and all the haul.
Pulling out the stops

say that it heave
our heart

for help and handy,
timely assistance

please. Look at
one – toil, another –

moil. Well together
we think we

work. We think
'Like Trojans' and

to think we thought
to say it. Hey!

4 *Ding Dong*

'Hay' was what
came to me as I cut

through it,
suddenly aware as I

stalked through
it that was

clearly field – and
sown, grown, mown –

you name it. Then,
philosophically,

you understand, I
understood, you

must be sure to name
the thing you know,

and if you don't know
it, no it, you know.

5 *Pooh Pooh*

No! Not 'field'
but felt. The first

stir of it needful,
hearty, hate or

angry shake to
clear the throat

and tongue of
something, something

clotting. And then
there is escape,

the hiss and built
pressure which

is felt, the feeling
raw. The roar

of this has bloomed
like light or flower.

6 *Musical*

Flower gave us choice:
convolvulus or heartsease?

Picked, I think
the second. For sound

and sentiment.
And song we did

then, mostly
to each other, but

with joy, we were
appealing, keening,

harking our utmost –
eyeing, concealing

nothing amid all.
Still it goes on,

from lilt, swing, trill,
bop, blues to hum.

NOTE: The nicknames *Gesture*, *Bow Wow*, *Yo He Ho*,
Ding Dong, *Pooh Pooh* and *Musical* all describe actual
theories of the origin of speech.

Tracey Herd

MOIRA CONWAY

TRACEY HERD was born in 1968 in East Kilbride but has lived on the east coast of Scotland for most of her life. Her poems shaded by film noir, fairytale and iconographic myth are compelling and unsettling studies of the beast within. She won an Eric Gregory Award in 1993 and a Scottish Arts Council Bursary in 1995. She went to university, lives and works in Dundee. ●

Selection from: *No Hiding Place* (1996 Bloodaxe).

Gia

In drugstores across America
on laminated cards at points-of-sale
her lips are the glistening focus,
freshly painted with Melon-Shine,
the season's new shade from Maybelline.
In magazines, she struggles against a fake storm
with an umbrella by Christian Dior.

New York: a seventies summer.
A small apartment, spartanly furnished.
The morning is already warm,
the windows flung wide open
to catch the sun's first sweet rush
before the sidewalks bake and crack.
On the cover of August's *Vogue*
the model's complexion is as flawless
as a fresh snowfall
and her eyes are open very wide
in a halo of mink and klieg lights.

Southampton, Long Island: a week-long shoot.
Her chestnut hair is piled high on her head.
She rests her bare feet on a rock
and her hands paddle in the sparkling blue water.
The tide slaps against the track-marks
that run from wrist to elbow.

She is prowling in a thin black dress
on the roof of a building two hundred feet up
in the heart of the garment district:
black stockings, heels, slant eyes, a scowl.
A freezing wind sways the building.

In the darkroom the pictures float
in their tray of developing-fluid.
The emerging face is defiant and sad.
The eyes are dead, the fabulous body
is stripped of its flesh.
He lifts out the bones of the drowned girl.

Pat Taffe and Arkle

> *Taffe was understandably amused by attempts*
> *to compare any latter-day chasers with Arkle.*
> *He was adamant that there would never be another*
> *horse like the Duchess of Westminster's champion.*
> TONY O'HEHIR, 1992

After the last exhausted horse
has stumbled past the winning-post
at Gowran Park, Dundalk and Fairyhouse
and the determined wind has uprooted
paper scraps and the thin covering of grass,
there is nowhere left for the eye to wander
beneath the black sky and the yellow stars.
The night carries your racing colours.

In the straw-strewn, cobbled stable-yard,
I am ringed by the bright nervous eyes
of the horses. I gather up the reins,
the leather cold and scuffed,
and settle myself into the creaking saddle.
Your ears are pricked, your eyes stare
straight ahead. If the truth be told
I had never quite come back to earth.

Big Girls

Granny's here. Her mother's voice was bright
with pleasure. She turned away in spite.
Hello, she mumbled and dropped her eyes back
to the book she was reading. It was a book
for Big Girls. The knowledge stuffed her
with pride. Granny could go to Hell:
she slept on an unsightly brown and orange
floral camp bed in her bedroom
and snored and littered her face creams
all over the spotless dressing table,
but when she left she gave her money
and then she smiled. *Have a pleasant journey home.*
Choosing could take all morning, but it was fun:
Endless Night, The Mirror Crack'd,
Cat Among the Pigeons, Sparkling Cyanide.

The Pink Rose Rings

She remembered seeing the underpass up ahead
and thinking how cool it would be when they slipped
into its shade. That was mere seconds before his hands
flew to the black hole in his throat. She turned
then, dazzled, the sun seeming to explode
beside her in the car. She remembered
the intricate pink rose rings in his skull, vivid
as the flowers that lay beside them on the seat,
and cradling his head, bewildered by the riot
of colour, wilting a little in the unseasonable heat.

Missing

By Monday morning it seems certain
that the chill of his absence
will be permanent.

This is his map
spread out on the counter-top,
imagine where he wandered

dizzy and frozen
along the death-route.
An invisible X marks the spot.

The Exhibits

In the museum of translucent
blue skins, the exhibits lie
soaking up the darkness, flat
as pricked balloons.

The girl with the bruised eyes
was unzipped from black plastic
and laid out
so that her parents could identify
what was no longer anybody's daughter.

On the Glittering Beaches

Growing tired of her hysterical gestures,
the way she wheeled and soared like a gull
round the cramped front room of their house,
he withdrew his presence, subtly at first:
a minute's silence when one word
was called for, a phone-call forgotten,
an eyebrow raised instead of an answer.

He turned his back when he came to bed,
later and later, ignoring the feeble creature
in one corner who'd smashed all her eggs
on the bare mattress springs and smeared
the spidery foetuses over her flesh.
She called to him from a great distance
as if searching the glittering beaches
of sleep in vain, for her mate.

Jane Holland

Selection from: *The Brief History of a Disreputable Woman* (1997 Bloodaxe).

JANE HOLLAND was born in Ilford in 1966. After university and a time living in France, she discovered, more or less by chance, a passion and a talent for snooker. She entered a man's world where the battle to overcome bigotted rules and attitudes was as great as the battle to perfect her own skills in the field. She has turned her formidable energies and gifts to poetry now with similarly turbulent and successful results. Jane Holland won an Eric Gregory Award in 1996. She lives on the Isle of Man, where she edits the poetry magazine *Blade*. ●

Pulse

Why should I speak of motherhood?
I might as well describe breathing
and have done with it.

Why should I eulogise breasts?
Have you never seen one?

Is my cunt so deliciously unusual,
it deserves three stanzas now
and a lifetime of comment?

We are no different from men,
except that a rapid pulse
beats hard at cunt and breast,

where a small white hand
can be seen emerging,
or clutching a fold of skin
like a love-letter, suckling.

I am not a woman poet.
I am a woman and a poet.
The difference is in the eyes.

Spin-Cycle

You've been blackberrying again.
I take your blouse
and watch it turn

through the white suds
in the drum, rinse-hold,
spinning slowly through the cycle.

I hear you up above,
bouncing on the bed
to reach the oval mirror,

see the purple stains
around your mouth and chin,
the blackness under nails

and in your hair.
Soon, like your swan-necked sister,
you will not have to stretch

on tip-toe for the sink
or grip the rail
when coming down the stairs.

You say 'when'.
I do not have the answers.
Just the slow loop

of your blouse
growing heavy with water,
as one cycle ends
and waits upon another.

Three Tests for Darwin Duke

I

When I was a kid, still in short trousers,
peeping through windows
to see the colour of my neighbour's underwear,
I wanted to be a fireman
and chase that red-faced bell-borne fire-truck
straight through the centre of town
like a hero, hell-spawned and almost eaten alive
by the wicked white tongue of a fire too hot for the hose,
shattering windows with the blunt edge of an axe,
rescuing women in their buttoned nightclothes,
hair loose and lightly singed on their shoulders
who were always extremely grateful afterwards.

But the Duke became a caretaker instead
before they kicked me out
for setting the alarm off once a week
so I could hang out the window
and watch those engines screaming in,
sirens blaring in the heat of the day
and those firemen riding its hot red sides
like the Horsemen of the Apocalypse.
Then I'd pull out of the crowd
some sweat-faced girl in pigtails
and tell her it was safest in the boiler room
where pipes fan down their long black tentacles
dripping with oil and full of the reek of darkness
and I'd feel her up against the wall
until she laughed, when I'd drop her back
by her class and go home to my own woman
who always smells like a side of bacon
and who often laughs too, but for a different reason.
I guess I never really wanted to be a fireman.

II

This is the Duke on the line again.
I'm spinning a yarn – are you following?
What's a boy to do with a mother like mine,
a woman who never ran away to join a circus in her life,
although she wanted to
once or twice, but never spoke it aloud
in case I took her at her word:
saw her, sequinned, hanging from a rope
in that billowing canvas,
the death-wish of a golden mane
bunched like a fistful of corn beneath her,
two steps back from the raised chair
of a tamer, but herself untamed
in that great tide of people roaring
the foot-stamp ring of their clapping,
yet she blinked that thought at me
three times under her eyelids,
on her knees in the dust of the yard, praying
or just scrubbing the doorstep.
She baked it into her meat and potato pies
and the rise of her home-made bread, like a secret
written in flour on her shining forehead,
bright and coarse from the heat of the oven
or the long slow slop of water on a scrubbing-board.
'Darwin,' she would say,
although my father christened me Albert,
'it's a short hard fall from the top
of the wash-house step,
so mind you never take it in the dark
or leap across it like your father did,
god rest his soul, carrying two chickens
and not thinking where his foot would fall.'

III

I said to myself: Darwin, one day
these people will understand where you're coming from.
They may not know where you're headed
but they'll get the gist of it.
Just put that slim blue flower behind your ear again
and sing those gentle songs of love:
the rushed-heart, the red-twist of a salmon jumping.
Who wants to hear about violence
when you can see that down the High Street
or in your living room, where you rise like the walking dead
and with that sleep-face white-torn look
admit to being no good in bed to your woman,
who is busy training your canary
to perform fellatio? But this is the Nineties.
There are machines for that now.

Darwin, let's face it –
out under the cold bright look of the stars
we are no nearer Nirvana.
The best we can do is smoke blow
and drink a little whisky on the side.
These words are only words.
They don't pay bills.
They don't make love for us,
like canaries can.
But if they act as a pause
between sleeping and waking,
if they wind firmly like a red thread
between your fingers, moving
and unmoving, and like that ancient
warning they are not heeded,
then you can sow that seed
in the deep sleep of innocence
and hush your woman's mouth
with it before morning.

Loco

There is a train,
an endless track of railroad in my head.

The tracks are overrun with seed,
they clamour with the scent of grass.

Beneath the bridge,
an arch of moss has taken hold.

The flags are up.
The whistle blows – three-thirty every day

– a ritual of steam and speed
and racing wind.

I fashioned you from singing-steel.
I hammered out a ring

that cooled in locomotive style.
I took your breath,

your cold indifference
and blew it through a tunnel

like an iron god –
the shriek, the whistle in the dark!

I am all talk,
all track.

I sway as grass
green-bent on gravel in the heat,

the fire of your passing,
steam-blown-white, unstoppable.

Jackie Kay

INGRID POLLARD

Selection from: *The Adoption Papers* (1991 Bloodaxe), *Other Lovers* (1993 Bloodaxe), and *Off Colour* (1998 Bloodaxe)

JACKIE KAY was born in Scotland in 1961. Her first collection, *The Adoption Papers*, tells the story, her story, of a black girl's adoption by a white Scottish couple. Her second book, *Other Lovers*, includes a sequence on the Blues singer, Bessie Smith. These narratives, told from different points of view, are typical of her brave, passionate and generous approach, her skill at putting herself in someone else's shoes and her fine and subtle imagination. She also writes for the stage, screen, for children and is just completing her first novel. She has won a Gregory Award, a Forward Prize, a Somerset Maugham Award, and the Signal Poetry Award. She lives in Manchester. ●

Even the trees

Even the trees outside feel it, their fine branches
their sixth sense of mercy,

they bend into the wind and ask for forgiveness
to come in a storm,

and join the congregation of silence; that tall witness.
One man, tied to a tree and whipped

never worked again in the cotton fields. In the early
light, the delicate bone-light

that broke hearts, a song swept from field to field;
a woman's memory paced centuries,

down and down, a blue song in the beat of her heart,
in an old car that crossed

a railroad track; the scream of a warning –
is that why we remember certain things and not others;

the sound of the bass, the sound of the whip, the strange
strangled wind, bruises floating through light air

like leaves and landing, landing, here; this place.
Everything that's happened once could happen again.

In my country

walking by the waters
down where an honest river
shakes hands with the sea,
a woman passed round me
in a slow watchful circle,
as if I were a superstition;

or the worst dregs of her imagination,
so when she finally spoke
her words spliced into bars
of an old wheel. A segment of air.
Where do you come from?
'Here,' I said, 'Here. These parts.'

Crown and Country

When you come to our country
you will realise we are big on dentistry:
at the border your mouth will be opened, flossed
and an elegant silver filling stamped into D10.
Then you will catch the hygienic autobus, *Tooth
Fairy Express* smiling the improved smile of our people

who all know dentures are more crucial
than culture. We do not talk much, we say
cheese; pints of creamy gleaming teeth,
pouring out our white grins, our gold caps; smirks.
Just across the border, people have hellish holes,
gaping gaps, rotten roots, abscesses.

We identify people by their bite.
The lower class have most unusual bites.
They are sick to the back teeth.
At 2 a.m. on a hot dusty night in our town
you will hear the fraught percussion
of the entire population grinding its teeth.

Our dentists are the richest in the world,
mining our gobs of gold. They love the old;
the ones who finally succumb to receding gums,
to teeth falling haplessly out like hailstones.
Be careful of the wind; it can make your mouth fly wide.
All along this natural canal, you will note,
our wild poppies pout; lush red lips.

Virus [2]

The mice come first. In our bedroom
at the top of the house we hear the cunning
scraping, scuttling inside the skirting.
It is the first sign.

The plague of flies are next. In our kitchen
at the bottom of the house, they swarm in sick
thick circles. It is late October.
The Pied Piper calls. 'Something big,' he says.
'Must be something big and rotten.

Look for the eggs, tiny, white.'
This is the time of the Wests.
'Do you mean a body?' you say, anxious.
The Dalston train thunders by like fury

at the bottom of our town garden.
And yesterday the wasps came.
Two thousand strong. An army in my study
and the wee toilet. The Pied Piper returns.
'Vicious bastards,' his eyes gleam with job satisfaction.

This is our love nest. I see you, looking at me.

Maw Broon Visits a Therapist

Crivens! This is jist typical.
When it comes tae talking aboot masel
I jist clam up. Canny think whit
tae say.

Weel, weel. I'm here because
I canny hawnle life, ken whit I mean
because everything is awfy
and I'm no masel.

I dinny ken who Maw Broon is anymare.
I canny remember my Christian name.
I remember when I wis a bairn
folks cried me something.

The idea o' me ever being a bairn
is no right noo. A feel I've aye worn
this same pinnie and this heid scarf
I've got on the noo.

How come you've no got anything tae say?
You've no opened yir mooth.
Whit's wrang. Am A no daeing it right.
I dinny ken hoo yir supposed tae dae therapy.

Jings. Dae A jist talk on like this.
Michty. This is awfy awkward.
You've no said a dickie bird.
Tell you a dream? Crivens,

I've no had a dream since I wis a wean.
An image? Whit kind of image?
What comes tae mind?
Whit represents whit?

Och. This therapy's making me crabbit.
I thought this wuid gie me a wee lift.
This is awfy. I feel unweel.
How dae I see masel?

Weel. I'm fed up wey ma bun.
It is jist a big onion
at the back o' ma heid.
I canny let ma hair doon.

I'm built like a two-ton tank.
I'm constantly wabbit and crabbit.
A' anybody sees is Maw Broon.
I'll aye be the wan tae dae it

whitever 'it' is. Here – I'm quite guid
at this therapy lark eh?
I could dae this masel.
Sit there like you are, glaikit

a box o' tissues and a clock
and a few wee emmms and aaas.
Jings, it's money for old rope.
There that's whit I feel like –

a tatty old rope
nibiddy wuid want tae climb
a' twistit and tangled
an, jings, this is exciting

I could break. I could jist give in.

Pounding Rain

News of us spreads like a storm.
The top of our town to the bottom.
We stand behind curtains
parted like hoods; watch each other's eyes.

We talk of moving to the west end,
this bit has always been a shoe box
tied with string; but then again
your father still lives in that house

where we warmed up spaghetti bolognese
in lunch hours and danced to Louis Armstrong,
his gramophone loud as our two heart beats
going boom diddy boom diddy boom.

Did you know then? I started dating Davy;
when I bumped into you I'd just say Hi.
I tucked his photo booth smile into my satchel
brought him out for my pals in the intervals.

A while later I heard you married Trevor Campbell.
Each night I walked into the school dinner hall
stark naked, till I woke to Miss, Miss Miss
every minute. Then, I bumped into you at the Cross.

You haven't changed you said; that reassurance.
Nor you; your laugh still crosses the street.
I trace you back, beaming, till –
Why don't you come round, Trevor would love it.

He wasn't in. I don't know how it happened.
We didn't bother with a string of do you remembers.
I ran my fingers through the beads in your hair.
Your hair's nice I said stupidly, nice, suits you.

We sat and stared till our eyes filled
like a glass of wine. I did it, the thing
I'd dreamt a million times. I undressed you
slowly, each item of clothing fell

with a sigh. I stroked your silk skin
until we were back in the Campsies, running
down the hills in the pounding rain,
screaming and laughing; soaked right through.

Mimi Khalvati

MIMI KHALVATI was born in Tehran in 1944. She was educated in Switzerland and the UK and worked for some years as a director and actor in Tehran. Her lyrical, supple intelligence sifts her experience of the Iranian diaspora, childhood memories, contemporary concerns of the family and of East-West relations and makes a clear personal sense of it. She lives in London with her children. ●

Selection from: *In White Ink* (1991 Carcanet), *Mirrorwork* (1995 Carcanet).

On Reading Rumi

Earlier, to be ready, I hoovered the carpet.
Fluff from your socks has strewn it like cotton-flowers.
I pick them, spin them to thread between my fingers.
Short threads. Where are you now?

*

Night is not the death of day. It is
her lying-in, her waters breaking. Why
not stay then? Ease her way? A new day,
stillborn, will only multiply our miseries.

*

Night, so you let us sleep *like fish in black water*!
Sluggish, I slow-nibble, stare. When I move,
my Master's line moves with me. Far above,
he is sleeping like a rock; too drunk to stir.

*

If, as you say, when I feel my *lips becoming*
infinite and sweet, when I feel *that spaciousness inside,*
Shams of Tabriz will be there too, please tell him,
graciously, two is company, three's a crowd.

*

My friend has broken up with her own friend –
and he's no Guide, whose lines might make amends.
If guidelines could, I'd give her, as a token –
the egg is whole, though the shell be broken.

*

Why should I listen when skin is more persuasive?
Or touch, when looking without touching can give
a taste of love so unlooked for, and so rare?
Today, your scent. Gratefulness rises on the air.

(Quotations are from *Quatrains of Rumi, Unseen Rain,*
translated by John Moyne & Coleman Barks)

Rubaiyat
(for Telajune)

Beyond the view of crossroads ringed with breath
her bed appears, the old-rose covers death
has smoothed and stilled; her fingers lie inert,
her nail-file lies beside her in its sheath.

The morning's work over, her final chore
was 'breaking up the sugar' just before
siesta, sitting cross-legged on the carpet,
her slippers lying neatly by the door.

The image of her room behind the pane,
though lost as the winding road shifts its plane,
returns on every straight, like signatures
we trace on glass, forget and find again.

I have inherited her tools: her anvil,
her axe, her old scrolled mat, but not her skill;
and who would choose to chip at sugar-blocks
when sugar-cubes are boxed beside the till?

The scent of lilacs from the road reminds me
of my own garden: a neighbouring tree
grows near the fence. At night its clusters loom
like lantern-moons, pearly-white, unearthly.

I don't mind that the lilac's roots aren't mine.
Its boughs are, and its blooms. It curves its spine
towards my soil and litters it with dying
stars: deadheads I gather up like jasmine.

My grandmother would rise and take my arm,
then sifting through the petals in her palm
would place in mine the whitest of them all:
'Salaam, dokhtaré-mahé-man, salaam!'

'Salaam, my daughter-lovely-as-the-moon!'
Would that the world could see me, Telajune,
through your eyes! Or that I could see a world
that takes such care to tend what fades so soon.

Blue Moon

Sitting on a windowsill, swinging
her heels against the wall as the gymslips
circled round and Elvis sang Blue Moon,

she never thought one day to see her daughter,
barelegged, sitting crosslegged on saddlebags
that served as sofas, pulling on an ankle

as she nodded sagely, smiling, not denying:
you'll never catch me dancing to the same old tunes;
while her brother, strewed along a futon,

grappled with his Sinclair, setting up
a programme we had asked him to. Tomorrow
he would teach us how to use it, but for now

he lay intent, pale, withdrawn, peripheral
in its cold white glare as we went up to our rooms:
rooms we once exchanged, like trust, or guilt,

each knowing hers would serve the other better
while the other's, at least for now, would do.
The house is going on the market soon.

My son needs higher ceilings; and my daughter
sky for her own Blue Moon. You can't blame her.
No woman wants to dance in her Mum's old room.

Stone of Patience

'In the old days,' she explained to a grandchild bred in England,
'in the old days in Persia, it was the custom to have a stone,
a special stone you would choose from a rosebed, or a goat-patch,
a stone of your own to talk to, tell your troubles to,
a stone we called, as they now call me, a stone of patience.'

No therapists then to field a question with another,
but stones from dust where ladies' fingers, cucumbers
curled in sun. Were the ones they used for gherkins
babies that would have grown, like piano tunes had we known
the bass beyond the first few bars? Or miniatures?

Some things I'm content to guess: colour in a calyx-tip,
is it gold or mauve? A girl or a boy... Patience
was so simple then: waiting for the clematis to open,
to purple on a wall; the bud to shoot out stamens,
thc jet of milk to leave its rim like honey

on the bee's fur. But patience when the cave is sealed,
a boulder at the door, is riled by the scent of hyacinth
in the blue behind the stone: the willow by the pool
where once she sat to trim a beard with kitchen scissors,
to tilt her hat at smiles, at sleep, at congratulations.

And a woman, faced with a lover grabbing for his shoes
when women-friends would have put themselves in hers,
no longer knows what's virtuous. Will anger shift
the boulder, buy her freedom, and the earth's? Or patience,
like the earth's, be abused? Even nonchalance

can lead to courage, to conception: a voice that says
oh come on darling, it'll be all right, oh do let's.
How many children were born from words such as these?
I know my own were; now learning to repeat them, to outgrow
a mother's awe of consequences her body bears.

So now that midsummer, changing shape, has brought in
another season, the grape becoming raisin, hinting
in a nip at the sweetness of a clutch, one fast upon another:
now that the breeze is raising sighs from sheets
as she tries to learn again, this time for herself,

to fling caution to the winds like colour in a woman's skirt
or to borrow patience from the stones in her own backyard
where fruit still hangs on someone else's branch…don't ask her
whose? as if it mattered. Say: *they won't mind*
as you reach for a leaf, for the branch, and pull it down.

Needlework

Within the lamplight's radius,
within the frame the flowers,
my name within my lifetime
handed on to no one dies with me.

My knots are neat.
My cottage gardens will be stretched
with the ones my daughters stitch.
My youngest keeps me company.

On an upper landing where my work
is hung, in another century,
some strange and foreign woman
may try to picture me

and fail. Or is that I fail
to picture her? I cannot think
what she would want with me.
With hollyhocks and bonnets.

Gwyneth Lewis

GWYNETH LEWIS was born in Cardiff in 1959. She writes and publishes in both Welsh, her first language, and in English. Her poetry is full of mysteries, some of them divine, a shimmering originality, all reined in by her command of form and by a tough, demanding intelligence. She won an Eric Gregory Award in 1988. Her first book was shortlisted for the Forward Prize for Best First Collection and won the Aldeburgh Poetry Festival Prize. She works in Cardiff as a television producer. ●

TIM BRETT

Selection from: *Parables & Faxes* (1995 Bloodaxe) and and *Zero Gravity* (1998 Bloodaxe).

Pentecost

The Lord wants me to go to Florida.
I shall cross the border with the mercury thieves,
as foretold in the faxes and prophecies,
and the checkpoint angel of Estonia
will have alerted the uniformed birds
to act unnatural and distract the guards

so I pass unhindered. My glossolalia
shall be my passport – I shall taste the tang
of travel on the atlas of my tongue –
salt Poland, sour Denmark and sweet Vienna
and all men in the Spirit shall understand
that, in His wisdom, the Lord has sent

a slip of a girl to save great Florida.
I shall tear through Europe like a standing flame,
not pausing for long, except to rename
the occasional city; in Sofia
thousands converted and hundreds slain
in the Holy Spirit along the Seine.

My life is your chronicle; O Florida
revived, look forward to your past,
and prepare your perpetual Pentecost
of golf course and freeway, shopping mall and car
so the fires that are burning in the orange groves
turn light into sweetness and the huddled graves

are hives of the future – an America
spelt plainly, translated in the Everglades
where palm fruit hang like hand grenades
ready to rip whole treatises of air.
Then the S in the tail of the crocodile
will make perfect sense to the bibliophile

who will study this land, his second Torah.
All this was revealed. Now I wait for the Lord
to move heaven and earth to send me abroad
and fulfil His bold promise to Florida.
As I stay put, He shifts His continent:
Atlantic closes, the sheet of time is rent.

Flyover Elegies
(for Jane)

I

The traffic's been worse than ever this year,
straining bumper to choking tail,
inching towards the roundabout. We feel
that there's less oxygen to breathe in air,

less room for manoeuvre. The flyover's arch
holds cars in a rainbow whose pot of gold's
somewhere in town. Meantime, below,
mothers with pushchairs use the underpass,

struggle with shopping. These are the circles
of Dante's hell. There's the view
from the parapet, of course. But you,
like the traffic, wanted somewhere else.

II

Pain made you a cow,
though certain men
liked that suffering in you,

at least for a while. That ache
drove you to lying and then on
with hope to the next regrettable mistake

involving kissing. Your heart
went missing. You searched
in all the wrong places, carried a note

by yet another bloke
who said that he loved you,
till that burning lack

inside you drove even he away.
Love's never enough. As for his words,
you never believed them anyway.

III

I remember the flyover being built.
The word was for freedom, for rising high
and swiftly over the heavy wait
of junction. It was for cruising, it was for view,
it was for ease of passing through.

It sounded like death. All day the pile-
drivers thudded into the earth
with a horrible heartbeat. Flying takes depth
and violence. You knew as you leapt.
Now the overpass stands, your monument.

IV

At two in the morning the strongest hug
never touches the hurt. A mug

looks promising, but delivers less
than a bottle. Now the breath's

a faithless friend who's disappeared,
comes back in the nick of time. Tears

are diamond earrings. You crave
some rightness, but you don't believe

anything less than pain: the tug
of concrete with its credible hug.

V

I think of you as I'm changing gear,
approaching the junction. Sign:
All Through Traffic. Industrial Estate.
Cardiff City Centre. In their cars,

wrapped in their music, the commuters glide,
profiles pharaonic on the sunset's tomb.
A470. M4 West. Illness had made
you less than yourself. When you died

you became much larger. Now you wear
the roundabout like a sparkling belt,
rush-hour traffic like chiffon scarves.
I see your foot in the welcoming air,

hold it there, precious. Forget the shame
of failing, we all know your fall
as we plunge ourselves, daily, clutching the wheel,
grateful today that we're driving home.

Advice on Adultery

(FROM *Welsh Espionage*)

The first rule is to pacify the wives
if you're presented as the golden hope
at the office party. You're pure of heart,
but know the value of your youthful looks.
Someone comments on your lovely back.
Talk to the women, and avoid the men.

In work they treat you like one of the men
and soon you're bored with the talk of the wives
who confide in you about this husband's back,
or that husband's ulcer. They sincerely hope
you'll never have children...it ruins your looks.
And did you know David has a dicky heart?

You go to parties with a beating heart,
start an affair with one of the men.
The fact you've been taking good care of your looks
doesn't escape the observant wives
who stare at you sourly. Cross your fingers and hope
that no one's been talking behind your back.

A trip to the Ladies. On your way back
one of them stops you for a heart to heart.
She hesitates, then expresses the hope
that you won't take offence, but men will be men,
and a young girl like you, with such striking looks....
She's heard nasty rumours from some of the wives.

She knows you're innocent, but the wives,
well, jump to conclusions from the way it looks....
In a rage, you resolve she won't get him back,
despite the pressure from the other wives.
They don't understand... you'll stick with the men,
only they are *au fait* with affairs of the heart.

You put it to him that you're living in hope.
He grants that you're beautiful, but looks
aren't everything. He's told the men,
who smirk and wink. So now you're back
to square one, but with a broken heart.
You make your peace with the patient wives.

Don't give up hope at the knowing looks.
Get your own back, have a change of heart:
Ignore the men, start sleeping with the wives.

The Hedge

With hindsight, of course, I can see that the hedge
was never my cleverest idea
and that bottles of vodka are better not wedged

like fruit in its branches, to counter the fears
and the shakes in the morning on the way to work.
Looking back, I can see how I pushed it too far

when I'd stop in the lay-by for a little lurk
before plunging my torso in, shoulder high
to the hedgerow's merciful root-and-branch murk

till I'd felt out my flattie and could drink in the dry
and regain my composure with the cuckoo-spit.
Then, with growing wonder, I'd watch the fungi,

lovely as coral in the aqueous light.
Lovely, that is, till that terrible day
when the hedge was empty. Weakened by fright

I leant in much deeper to feel out which way
the bottle had rolled and, cursing my luck
(hearing already what my bosses would say

about my being caught in this rural ruck),
I started to panic, so I tussled and heaved
and tried to stand upright, but found I was stuck.

I struggled still harder, but you'd scarcely believe
the strength in a hedge that has set its mind
on holding a person in its vice of leaves

and this one was proving a real bind.
With a massive effort, I took the full strain
and tore up the hedgerow, which I flicked up behind

me, heavy and formal as a wedding train.
I turned and saw, to my embarrassment,
that I'd pulled up a county with my new-found mane,

which was still round my shoulders, with its tell-tale scent
of loam and detritus, while trunk roads and streams
hung off me like ribbons. It felt magnificent:

minerals hidden in unworked seams
shone like slub silver in my churned-up trail.
I had brooches of newly built housing schemes

and sequins of coruscating shale;
power-lines crackled as they changed their course
and woodsmoke covered my face like a veil.

Only then did I feel the first pangs of remorse.
Still, nobody'd noticed so, quickly, I knelt,
took hold of the landscape, folded and forced

it up to a chignon which I tied with my belt.
It stayed there, precarious. The occasional spray
of blackthorn worked loose, but I quickly rebuilt

the ropey construction and tucked it away.
Since then I've become quite hard to approach:
I chew mints to cover the smell of decay

which is with me always. Food tastes of beech
and I find that I have to concentrate
on just holding the hairstyle since it's started to itch

and the people inside it are restless of late.
Still, my tresses have won me a kind of renown
for flair and I find my hair titillates

certain men who want me to take it down
in front of them, slowly. But with deepening dread
I'm watching my old self being overgrown

while scruples rustle like quadrupeds,
stoat-eyed, sharp-toothed in my tangled roots
(it's so hard to be human with a hedge on your head!).

Watch me. Any day I'll be bearing fruit,
sweet hips that glint like pinpricks of blood
and my dry-land drowning will look quite cute

to those who've never fallen foul of wood.
But on bad days now I see nothing but hedge,
my world crazed by the branches of should,

for I've lost all centre, have become an edge
and though I wear my pearls like dew
I feel that I've paid for my sacrilege

as I wish for my autumn with its broader view.
But for now I submit. With me it will die,
this narrowness, this slowly closing eye.

Sarah Maguire

SARAH MAGUIRE was born in London in 1957. She trained as a gardener straight from school and later studied at the universities of East Anglia and Cambridge. She writes dark, erotic, complex and lyrical poems which are so richly layered you can almost taste them. Sarah Maguire was selected for the New Generation poetry promotion in 1994. She works freelance as a writer and broadcaster and lives in London. ●

CRISPIN HUGHES

Selection from: *Spilt Milk* (1991 Secker), *The Invisible Mender* (1997 Jonathan Cape).

The Divorce Referendum

Here it's a fortnight to Carnival.
On hot nights I lie outside the sheets, listening to
the steel-bands practising till dawn – the throats

of oil-drums beaten to chromatics, glistening in the dark.
When it rains the railway seems to move
up the street – train after train slipping westwards

from Paddington, thickening the night.
You left from platform three. I leaned over the barrier,
my hands pressed together as if in prayer.

When you rang I was still wet from the bath. After ten years'
silence you realise how you love me. I touch you
and a vessel in your feminine nose gives way –

blood and your salt-sweet tears flood my fingers and lips.
Later my own blood inscribes the fresh sheets –
the scarlet letter, a map of desire nothing can shift.

In three months you'll leave Dublin. You tell me
the Divorce Referendum has made you choose exile.
In Camden Town you weigh a pint of Guinness in your palm,

drain it, push away the glass. I trace the rings
of beer-stains on the table with my finger,
or smoke your cigarettes right down to the stub.

Somewhere between here and Dún Laoghaire the boat broke down.
For hours you drift in the eye of your storm.
Leaning from a railing into stillness

you watch the amber light of the ferry fall into the night,
your eyes stinging from their search for a harbour.
Later you will write, *Perhaps I am still at sea.*

On the phone your voice is sallow with exhaustion,
its timbre frayed by a line carried miles under water.
When your daughter calls out in her sleep you must leave

to comfort her. I'll lie here now till dawn, twisting
the phone-cord round my fingers till my nails turn white,
longing for suffrage, for your casting vote.

Spilt Milk

Two soluble aspirins spore in this glass, their mycelia
fruiting the water, which I twist into milkiness.
The whole world seems to slide into the drain by my window.

It has rained and rained since you left, the streets black
and muscled with water. Out of pain and exhaustion you came
into my mouth, covering my tongue with your good and bitter milk.

Now I find you have cashed that cheque. I imagine you
slipping the paper under steel and glass. I sit here in a circle
of lamplight, studying women of nine hundred years past.

My hand moves into darkness as I write, *The adulterous woman
lost her nose and ears; the man was fined.* I drain the glass.
I still want to return to that hotel room by the station

to hear all night the goods trains coming and leaving.

The Invisible Mender
(My First Mother)

I'm sewing on new buttons
to this washed silk shirt.
Mother of pearl,
I chose them carefully.
In the haberdashers on Chepstow Place
I turned a boxful over
one by one,
searching for the backs with flaws:
those blemished green or pink or aubergine,
small birth marks on the creamy shell.

These afternoons are short,
the sunlight buried after three or four,
sap in the cold earth.
The trees are bare.
I'm six days late.
My right breast aches so
when I bend to catch a fallen button
that strays across the floor.
Either way,
there'll be blood on my hands.

Thirty-seven years ago you sat in poor light
and sewed your time away,
then left.
But I'm no good at this:
a peony of blood
gathers on my thumb, falls
then widens on the shirt
like a tiny, opening mouth.

I think of you like this –
as darkness comes,
as the window that I can't see through
is veiled with mist
which turns to condensation
slipping down tall panes of glass,
a mirror to the rain outside –

and I know that I'll not know
if you still are mending in the failing light,
or if your hands (as small as mine)
lie still now, clasped together, underground.

Communion

I

We both might wonder what you're doing here
till you take refuge from your hunger in my fridge
and then come out with something

that we share the name for: *Choriço picante.*
I watch you pierce
the raw meat with a fork

and hold it in the naked ring of gas
until the skin is charred and blistered black
until the stove enamel's measled red.

Slit it down the side
and open out its bleeding heart -
ruddy, vivid, rough.

II

We cannot speak each other's tongue
and so you open up your shirt
to give me signs, to show your wounds.

I know this much:
that, as a child, you fled to Lisbon from Luanda
with a bayonet wound a foot long

(never sutured)
that now grows on your arm
as though a snake's embossed there;

that your skin was punched with shot
which, ten years later, form the dark stigmata
branded on your legs and arms.

III

Take this pungent flesh into your mouth
and staunch your hunger.
Eat.

Sinéad Morrissey

SINÉAD MORRISSEY was born in Portadown in 1972. She was educated in Belfast and Dublin. Her poetry is concerned with memory, love, death and the implications and complications of religious faith in a secular age. In 1990 she received the Patrick Kavanagh Award for poetry, the youngest poet ever to be honoured in this way. In 1996 she won an Eric Gregory Award. She lives and teaches in Japan. ●

Selection from: *There Was Fire in Vancouver* (1996 Carcanet).

There Was Fire in Vancouver

There was fire in Vancouver,
And we leaned out into the night to watch it
Set light to the East End.
It had taken stand on Commercial Avenue.

We marvelled at the darkness of the city,
All neon dulled by the superior flame,
And wondered would it bestow its dance
On the Ginseng Teahouse in Chinatown, on Jericho Pier.

There were no sirens, hoses, buckets even,
Scattering streets and 'Fire!' 'Fire!'
We seemed the only ones conscious of the bright crusade
And we watched with Moses standing in our heads.

My New Angels

God's old angels made us peaceful.
They had wings of love and explanation.
They brought us our destiny to lower our eyes
And let everything be for a reason.
There was no bewildering them.

My new angels are howling, hard,
And there are masses in heaven
For every snuffed out light on a back road.
Their rage is assured, ragged, unforgiving.
There is no perfecting them.

Thoughts in a Black Taxi

1

Four days to go until the twelfth, and the bonfire is fourteen feet high.
I want the driver to drive ten times around the diamond.
I've been gone too long –
I want to stare and stare.

I imagine winding my way through the *Dump Wood Here* signs
And the fallout of black tyres,
Dismantled shelving and donated sofas
To the bare-chested men swanking about on top.

Fascinated by the organisation,
I want to ask them where they got their ladders from.
One 'What are *You* called?' from them, and it would all go black.
I'd have to run to stay whole.

2

It's not as though I haven't blundered before –
Asking what UYM means by the Rushpark estate,
Or laughing at how the Germans think Paisley is mad
In a taxi heading east of the city.

I never registered thrown looks for hours afterwards.
My father sweated.
Even ordering I get it wrong these days –
This rank is UVF-run. Never say Morrissey again.

3

My teeth were so crooked it took six months at the Royal Victoria
Before I could smile without denting my lower lip.
Six years of the Grosvenor Road in a state high school uniform
Was like having *Protestant* slapped across your back.

I always walked with my heart constricting,
Half-expecting bottles, in sudden shards
Of West Belfast sunshine,
To dance about my head.

After the Hurricane

You saw the wind as the breath of God.
You couldn't help it. Your refusal of the ether
That would mist over death got smashed to splinters
Like the Florida coastline, up-ended in rain.
There was too much rage in the sky for it not to be God's.

Perhaps it was your position under the window,
At the mercy of whatever startled missile
Made its appearance next –
A tree, a house, a woman –
Over your head. You saw a shower of cars

Spat out like sycamore seeds
And a landscape that trailed wires
In its rush to be pure.
You felt too temporary not to be answerable
To the power in the break-up of hills.

Hazel Goodwin Morrissey Brown

I salvaged one photograph from the general clear-out, plucked
(Somehow still dripping) from the river of my childhood.
You in your GDR-Worker phase, salient, rehabilitated:
Reagan, you can't have your Banana Republic and eat it!
Your protest banner and your scraped back hair withstood the flood.
I've hung your smile beside your latest business card: *Nuskin Products.*

Contact address: Titirangi, New Zealand. Out there a psychic
Explained how, in a previous life, I'd been your mother,
Guillotined during the French Revolution. You were my albino son.
You saw fire in the windows. This time round we returned to the
          garrison –
Swanned round Paris in the summer playing guess-your-lover.
I wonder how many of our holidays have closed down cycles.

Anyway, I believe it. Because when you drove to the airport
And didn't come back, it was déjà vu. And I had to fight,
As all mothers do, to let you go. Our lived-in space
Became a house of cards, and there was nothing left to do but race
For solid ground. You settled your feathers after the flight
In a fairytale rainforest. Discovered the freedom of the last resort.

To Look Out Once from High Windows

Cost you your railway lines, washing lines, sex on billboards
Seven feet high, pissing in gardens, smoking in bedsits, dust.
Cost you the choice you never made so you could be lost
In the closest way to being found: the quicksand of a wife, in-laws,
The decrease that children bring, or an attic full of yourself only
Only yourself and only as you tell it – wanking and lonely.

Underneath your choice lay the surest way of being found:
To pass all the marriages, births, and seaside hols by
On an express train through life that doesn't stop. It was the honesty
Of death you wanted. Its silence was stunning, like the white surround
Of an all-round prison wall. The way life broke down to enter it was
            what
You couldn't bear, making young girls' summer photographs so falsely
            stopped

And irretrievable. To look out once from High Windows was to fly
Over the walls you saw in life, in life's renunciation
And beyond, and to accept that endlessness might mean resolution.
All words broke there. You stopped your various desolations colliding
By just looking up. You built your runway out of decimated love
And saw in flight how nothing could be left to lose or prove.

Alice Oswald

ALICE OSWALD was born in 1966. She read Classics at Oxford and then trained as a gardener at Wisley. She cites Homer, Dante, Ovid and the sculptor Barbara Hepworth as amongst her most important influences. Her poetry is musical, mysterious, full of a devotional passion for the natural world cast in a vivid language of singular clarity. In 1994 she won an Eric Gregory Award. In 1996 she was awarded the Arts Foundation's Poetry Fellowship, and her first book was given a Poetry Book Society Choice as well as being shortlisted for both the T.S. Eliot Prize and the Forward Prize for Best First Collection. ●

Selection from: *The Thing in the Gap-Stone Stile* (1996 OUP).

Mountains

Something is in the line and air along edges,
which is in woods when the leaf changes
and in the leaf-pattern's gives and gauges,
the water's tension upon ledges.
Something is taken up with entrances,
which turns the issue under bridges.
The moon is between places.
An outlet fills the space between two horses.

Look through a holey stone. Now put it down.
Something is twice as different. Something gone
accumulates a queerness. Be alone.
Something is side by side with anyone.

And certain evenings, something in the balance
falls to the dewpoint where our minds condense
and then inslides itself between moments
and spills the heart from its circumference;
and this is when the moon matchlessly opens
and you can feel by instinct in the distance
the bigger mountains hidden by the mountains,
like intentions among suggestions.

The Pilchard-Curing Song
(adapted from the Cornish of John Boson)

I sing of pilchards, caught on a rod
in the Bay of the Grey Rock in the wood.
'Tithe! Tithe!' Over the sea
the boats come home to a cry on the quay;
every big woman, with her bum upwards,
swinging away with a creel of pilchards.
Back at home, it's a day's turn
crying 'Holan moy for my hern hern!'
and in a month they'll be salted dry;
then break them up and pull them away
and a dirty girl can give them a wash
till her hands come up as clean as the fish.
Put them bright in barrels, head to tail.
Your pilchard is a profitable sale.
Then look for a log of thirteen feet
and a heap of stones five hundredweight
and keep an eye on the slow continual
drip-drop of oil from the barrel.
This is the true way. This is your standard
top quality market pilchard.
Year upon year, the boats'll take
loads of them from the Gwavas Lake
and a north-east wind'll blow them far
to where the well-heeled foreigners are
and everywhere it's the same trouble:
more of poor people, less of rich people.

The Melon Grower

She concerned him,
but the connection had come loose.
They made shift with tiffs and silence.

He sowed a melon seed.
He whistled in the greenhouse.
She threw a slipper at him

and something jostled in the loam
as if himself had been layed blind.
She misperceived him. It rained.

The melon got eight leaves, it lolled.
She banged the plates.
He considered his fretful webby hands.

'If I can sex' he said 'the flowers,
very gently I'll touch their parts
with a pollen brush made of rabbit hairs.'

The carpels swelled. He had to prop them on pots.
She wanted the house repainting.
He was out the back watering.

He went to church, he sang 'O Lord how long shall the wicked...?'
He prayed, with his thumbs on his eyes.
His head, like a melon, pressured his fingers.

The shoots lengthened
and summer mornings came with giant shadows
and arcs as in the interim of a resurrection.

She stayed in bed, she was coughing.
He led the side-shoots along the wires.
She threw the entire tea-trolley downstairs.

And when the milk was off
and when his car had two flat tyres
and when his daughter left saying she'd had enough,

he was up a ladder hanging soft nets from the beam
to stop the fruit so labouring the stem.
The four globes grew big at ease

and a melony smell filled the whole place
and he caught her once, confused in the greenhouse,
looking for binder-twine. Or so she says.

Wedding

From time to time our love is like a sail
and when the sail begins to alternate
from tack to tack, it's like a swallowtail
and when the swallow flies it's like a coat;
and if the coat is yours, it has a tear
like a wide mouth and when the mouth begins
to draw the wind, it's like a trumpeter
and when the trumpet blows, it blows like millions...
and this, my love, when millions come and go
beyond the need of us, is like a trick;
and when the trick begins, it's like a toe
tiptoeing on a rope, which is like luck;
and when the luck begins, it's like a wedding,
which is like love, which is like everything.

Ballad of a Shadow

Take from me my voice and I shall voiceless go
to find you; take from me my face,
I'll treck the hills invisibly,
my strength, and I shall run but keep no pace.

Even in cities, take the sense with which I reason
and I shall seek, but close it in your heart,
keep this and forget this
and this, when we're apart,

will be the shadow game of love.
And I shall love in secret
and I shall love in crowds
and love in darkness, in the quiet

outlet of shadows, and in cities
as a ghost walking unnoticed,
and love with books, using their pages like a wind,
not reading, and with people, latticed

by words but through the lattice loving.
And when at last my love is understood,
with you I shall not love but breathe
and turn by breathing into flesh and blood.

Ruth Padel

CHRIS ANDREWES

RUTH PADEL researched Greek tragedy, religion and psychology in Oxford, Paris, Berlin and Athens. She has had a variety of occupations from teaching ancient Greek to singing in an Istanbul nightclub. Her poetry is playful, erotic and finely intelligent, weaving history, myth and personal experience. Her second collection was a Poetry Book Society Recommendation. She has published studies of ancient Greek religion and modern psychology (with Princeton University Press), and is now writing a book on desire (for Faber). She lives in London with her daughter. ●

Selection from: *Summer Snow* (1990 Hutchinson), *Angel* (1993 Bloodaxe), *Fusewire* (1996 Chatto), *Touch and Go* (1998 Chatto).

On the Line

Feel, you said. *How does this feel?*
Shy, if you must know,
to be asked.

But after, when you'd left
this all-gold absence

round me, in me, in even my ears,
I wondered. Sharp,
an axe on a bell.

Blast of the *Trovatore* chorus
when you open the oven door.

An extra-terrestrial
skiffle in the dish
at Jodrell Bank.

As if I'd never known red.
Hi-volt chillies
doing press-ups in a haybag of velvet.

An anaconda with hiccups.
Like the only thing. Like you.

Tell Me About It

When they mourn you over there
the way you'd want, the way you mourn
your friends;

when they're celebrating
having loved you
in Derry, Rathmullen, wherever –

birettas, candles, Latin,
all the weavings you don't believe in
but love anyway and I'll never share

for who the hell converts to
ex-Catholic? – no one will know
someone's missing you here

for ever. Whose arms,
printed with that absolute
man's stillness

when your breath calms
into my shoulder and you fall asleep
inside me, open and close

in a foreign night round nothing.
Who misses the way
you pour loose change on the bar

in a puddle of fairytale silver
and move through the night,
through everything, curious,

mischievous as a mongoose,
and never an unkind word.
I might dream

of coming over, touching
just one friend's sleeve
to whisper

'Talk about him. A bit.
The way he was, here' –
but never do it. Instead

I'll say *Yes* in my sleep
to you. To no one. You'll put
your tongue in my mouth, deep,

the way you do,
and my eyes will open
on a dark garden. I'll wake up

touching myself for you.
The alarm will stare
venomous digits. I'll hang on

to the fragile haze
of a wine-bar
when you leant over the foreign formica,

haltering my hand within your two
like the filling in a sandwich,
sashaying the skin of each finger

down to the soft web between,
over and over, a rosary of rub
and slide, as if you could solder

me to your lifeline. As if
you could take me with you.
And I'll wish you had.

Trial

I was with Special Force, blue-X-ing raids
to OK surfing on the Colonel's birthday.
Operation Ariel: we sprayed Jimi Hendrix
loud from helis to frighten the slopes
before 'palming. A turkey shoot.

The Nang fogged up. The men you need
are moral and kill like angels. Passionless.
No judgement. Judgement defeats us.
You're choosing between nightmares all the time.
My first tour, we hissed into an encampment
early afternoon, round two. The new directive,

polio. Inoculating kids. It took a while.
As we left, this old man came up, pulled on our
back-lag jeep-hood, yacking. We went back.
They'd come behind us, hacked off
all the inoculated arms. There they were
in a pile, a pile of little arms.

Soon after, all us new recruits turned on
to angel-dust like the rest.
You get it subsidised out there.
The snail can't crawl on the straight
razor and live. I'm innocent.

Yew Berries

At my wedding he came over the grass
cupping them, drunk. 'Did you know
the thrill in your garden,
safe if you spit out the seed?
It's the flesh...' I half-thought
of Agatha Christie and taxine
but barely noticed. Why do I think of it now?
Did I dream a party at his place
years ago? A small brown bottle
in the bathroom, like (I now imagine)
what Romeo got hold of,
meant to make orgasm last:
'But it's lethal. A drop too much
and you're gone.' Red, promising,
my parents' sunny garden, a wedding.
Safe if you spit out the seed.
Why do I think of that now?

Angel

No one sees me. Fathoms up
a nest of rays, all protein,
grey velvet triangles

six metres wing to wing,
a coat on them like a Weimerana,
ripples at the edges, slow,

the way the skite-tooth grass
trembled in lunar winds back home.
So no one knows

and if they read the impress
where my egg sacs
crumbled into bed, work done,

there's nothing they could do.
I listen to the humming
and I wait. Suppose they clawed

one ring from my antenna-bone
up through that tunnel of sea-cow
and acetta-swabs

changing sex halfway through life,
pink to meridian blue,
they'd re-do Linnaeus,

any story of black holes,
re-assign prizes
for the signature of matter,

but still they wouldn't
see what's coming.
How do I know all this?

Baby, where I come from,
we had pre-rusted pictoscopes
to tell us about aliens like you.

Scotch

The fox you didn't know you had
in your front garden
is craning his velour neck

from the hedge at two in the morning
to see what he doesn't often
get a glimpse of,

that moonspark
on a glass of Scotch

he doesn't often smell
being more at home with fish-heads
and the rinds of Emmental:

trainspotting to his fox-astonishment
a tumbler doing the rounds of his own beat
about heart-height in the dark.

Katherine Pierpoint

R. SNOOK

KATHERINE PIERPOINT was born in 1961 in Northampton. She went to Exeter University and then worked in publishing and television. Her work is full of quirky narratives told in a richly textured language of great originality. In 1993 she was awarded a Hawthornden Castle International Creative Writing Fellowship. In 1996 she won a Somerset Maugham Award for *Truffle Beds*, and was also *Sunday Times* Young Writer of the Year. She lives and works as a freelance writer, editor and translator based in Cambridge. ●

Selection from: *Truffle Beds*
(1995 Faber).

In the Outhouse

Staying with a friend, you leave his mother's kitchen,
To walk the garden on an errand for herbs.
The wind snaps the drying sheets apart on the washing line
Giving sudden, triangular glimpses of a pond, and roses.

And here's an outhouse, with a scrap of frayed rush-matting on the
        red step;
A cool, stone-walled, flag-floored room,
Full of old buckets, coils of twine, garden tools,
A washing basket at a still but crazy angle with a peg-bag in its lap,
And there is a huge fridge with a split handle,
Industriously buzzing in the heavy half-light.
A certain – knack – with the handle,
And the inside suddenly shows ranked remains of meals –
Today's, then yesterday's, behind those the day before's,
And then a whole pile of dishes, badly-bundled clingfilm packets,
A tubular clot of cooked chicken livers,
And saucers with bones on. Natural relics.
A cold smell of cabbage, peppermint, blood and cream arises from
        the shelves.
Hurry back in sunlight with the green herbs for tonight's meal.

Combustion Engine

'The combustion engine is built on the principle
of a series of controlled explosions'

The street-traders were roaring and steaming,
Stuffing loose bananas rudely into bags,
Unpouching greasy pennies. Dogs stared,
Tomatoes rolled from boxes, and the busy roadside
Receded at once to a frieze
Intricate but still as a chain of paper dolls,
When the low-slung motorbike passed by;
Its spun-out note blown flat but steady.

Slow bullet, low throttle,
Loud with smoke and choke and oil;
Its combustion just contained
In the two raised fists of a silver, black and blue
Bearded rider. Dark-shaded eye of this smoky storm,
Cruising on the base of his spine,
Bootsoles, metal toecaps and lean, wide crotch first, advancing...

The small girl takes one step aside a moment
Under the peck and bob of her mother's basket.
She stands neatly, small socks level, feet together on the kerb,
One hand pressed under her collar, on the dry pucker of smocking –
And flips one quick, instinctive wave at him –
Matter-of-factly, just fingers moving. The biker passes,
Head of an invisible procession. Trawler of eyes,
Careless fisher of widening looks,
His backwash unfurls along the street.

Swim Right Up to Me

I first learnt to swim at home in my father's study
On the piano-stool, planted on the middle of the rug.
Stomach down, head up, arms and legs rowing hard;
I swam bravely, ploughing up the small room,
Pinned on a crushed stuckness of stomach to tapestry,
The twin handles hard on my elbows on the back-stroke.
A view down through four braced wooden legs
To the same thin spot in the rug.
My mother faced me, calling rhythmic encouragement,
Almost stepping back to let me swim up to her,
Reminding me to breathe;
And wiping my hair and eyes with her hand
As I swam and swam on the furniture against a running tide,
Pig-cheeked, concentrating on pushing and pushing away,
Planning to learn to fly next, easy,
Higher than the kitchen table, even. The garden wall.

Steeplejack

Entering the churchyard
I tread the stone steps' outer edge,
Hauling on the rail, to save their centres
Like an old wife with a new carpet.
On my back a heavy, soft clinking
Of oiled wooden handles and smooth iron,
Rolled and tied in warm leather;
I unsling the bag,
Place it clear of the white-flowered nettles.

Foxtail grasses crowd the graveyard wall,
Fidgeting in dusty sunlight.
Shafts of silver green, slow blend
Up through burgundy, to soft sandpuff of seeds.

A garden snail
Slides up a slim iris blade,
Feeling everything with its moist eye-tips,
Its shell a hardened whirlpool
Of concentration.

The job starts with
The moment of looking.
Send your eye up the spire
To hook to the top.
Lash your gaze to the weathercock's spurs
And unreel a rope back to the brain.
Assess the sides for footholds.
Take only tools you trust.
Leave the belfry shutters fastened back
When you start climbing
Straight up into the weather;
And then, when you come back,
It's easier. You're stepping in
From open light to dark –
The tricky part.

You only look the next inch up
Once each toe and finger and knee are wedged
Tight. Keep flat. Think flat, move one thought at a time.
Use your breathing like another limb.
Greet by private name each stone, each slate,
Each starblot of lichen,
Swept clean by rivers of air.

On windy days, the white air smashes round
Like a painting broken over you.
Your head's up through the back of the canvas;
Lookout in the ship of fools,
Skimmed by whirring swifts and swallows.

Never look around until the job is done.
Only wavered once in fifteen years of climbing;
A day of many weathers,
The wind in the hard north-east.
I'd just finished, spat out the last nail sideways,

Stowed away the hammer –
Then grasped the rope, and turned my face out, careful, to the land,
Slopes mixing green farms and bleakness...

And I thought, as slow as speaking,
All up from nowhere:
God – give this carpet – one good shake.
Let me leap up and out of it, for good.

The old man told me once on a bender
I was no better than a monkey,
Clinging to the spire like a mother's leg.
Thought of a picture I'd seen in lessons of
Screaming monkeys, mad with fleas,
All pout and yellow peg-teeth and crashing branches.
Old sod was shouting, thin-lipped round a jerking fag-end,
Waving his skinny arms about.
Looked just like a chimp's twin brother.

I'm quiet as a rule, don't say much.
Sometimes disappear a while
Once or twice, on the year-end.
Found astride the lychgate singing hymns,
The heavy padlock swinging empty,
Picked open like a startled crab in my fist.

Girls talk to me. More than to the priest,
With his fishwhite face upturned, away from them,
His dead black dress.
They tell their feelings to the man
Who climbs to the eye of the ginger sun;
And steps back to earth each time for the love of it.

Sometimes when I'm working at
Crawling up God's nose,
I think of the wooden egg I'm carving for my wife.
It's best walnut, seasoned;
Smoky whorls like tumbling clouds
Or good meat laced through with fat.
Fresh egg, heavy in the hand. Rocket-clean as a kiss
While cupping the back of the other head.

Deryn Rees-Jones

MOIRA CONWAY

DERYN REES-JONES was born in 1968. She did doctoral research on women poets at Birkbeck College, and her critical study, *Consorting with Angels: Modern Women Poets*, is published by Bloodaxe Books in 2002. Her poetry looks with great wit and verve at subjects and characters as different as a beloved Welsh grandma and a thirteen-stone transvestite who dreams of being Marilyn Monroe. She writes with a generous, sassy irony. In 1993 she won an Eric Gregory Award, and in 1996 received an Arts Council of England Writer's Award. She lives and works in Liverpool. ●

Selection from: *The Memory Tray* (1994 Seren), *Signs Round a Dead Body* (1998 Seren).

Making for Planet Alice

You stand on a chair with a wrinkled nose
In your glittery tiara. Queen Alice and her Queendom!

The room is full of ordinariness
And your laughter like a tossed coin

Spins into the air. Take me to that place, I say,
Where the trees grow upside-down and their thick bright roots

Explore the sky. Take me to that place
Over the backs of houses, past the forgotten railway,

Across the continents by rickshaw
Where the sun sets in a moment, then slowly rises

Like a blush. Where the door in the wall opens to yards
Of purple strawberries, a yellow field of grasshoppers –

Their low sweet hum. Where the green pool of your imagination
Laps the edges of your head like sleep, its yawning mountains

Rock like lullabies and clocks, and pampas grasses
Stroke your forehead in the winds. Quietly, quietly

Take me to that strange safe place, by bus, by unicycle
Helicopter, aeroplane. Let me sail to Planet Alice in my heart,

My leaky coracle; let me circumnavigate the moon,
The foam of snow-white stars. Take me to that strange place

That hurts me. That we both knew once upon a time.
Which I've not only lost, but forgotten how to say.

Service Wash

For six months now I've washed her clothes,
The old favourites, the new acquaintances:
One large bag of colours, one small bag of whites.
By now I've got to know the oyster camisole,
The chambray trouser suit, the pink silk blouse
That has its own expensive scent, the purple jogging suit
That smells of sweat and traffic. Her knickers
With the blood left on. Sometimes I think about her
And the way she does her hair, wanting to know
The thousand things about her that I don't already know.
The bell-boy says she's often out, that when he tips his hat
She smiles. My wife would kill me
If she knew the way I thought. *Pervert,*
She'd say. And then the rest. Perhaps she's right.
With the place to myself one afternoon
I tried a dress of hers, all fresh and newly ironed,
And then felt warm and close to her. I could have cried.
My breasts hung empty, huge pink satin flowers...

Mostly I keep myself to myself. Head down
And my back's covered. Christ knows, I need the job.
Sometimes, though, just sometimes, it can get too much and absent-
Mindedly I mismatch my clients' socks.
That gets them ringing for *Room service!*
Never her. I think she's like that, likes
To wear them odd. Once an old bloke
Sent me down a note which said that socks
Were Lost Platonic souls. I like the way that sounds.

Perhaps one day I'll say the same to her.
I'd love to make her laugh. Sometimes I see her smiling
Through the steam. Then she dissolves. Love's spectre.
There's no end to what you learn down here.

Sometimes I think an afternoon will last for ever.
Sometimes I think the world is flat. Go on. Convince me.
Sometimes I think I'll fall in love again.

I Know Exactly the Sort of Woman I'd Like to Fall in Love With

If I were a man.

And she would not be me, but
Older and graver and sadder.
And her eyes would be kinder;
And her breasts would be fuller;
The subtle movements
Of her plum-coloured skirts
Would be the spillings of a childhood summer.

She would speak six languages, none of them my own.

And I? I would not be a demanding lover.
My long fingers, with her permission
Would unravel her plaited hair;
And I'd ask her to dance for me, occasionally,
Half-dressed on the moon-pitted stairs.

And Please Do Not Presume

And please do not presume it was the way we planned it,
Nor later say *We might have tried harder,*
Or *Could have done better.*
Nor remind us of the things we didn't take:
The hints, the trains, the tonics,
The tape-recordings of ourselves asleep,
The letters of a previous lover,
The photos of each other as a child.

And please do not presume our various ways of making up,
Of telling lies and truths, the way we touched
Or laughed, the Great Mistakes, the Tiger Suit,
Our list of *Twenty Favourite Movie Classics,*
Breakfast in bed, red wine, the different ways we tried
To make each other come
Were anything else than the love we wanted;

Or that we did no more or less than anybody might have done.

And more, do not presume we could have stopped it –
Like a clock, a gap, a leak, or rot; or made it
Last much longer than it did;
Or that the note on the fridge that one of us left,
Wasn't sweetly meant, but badly spelt:
Step One of Ten Proggressive Ways to Disolution.

It Will Not Do

It will not do how stupidly you love her
and how stupidly that stops you loving me.
How my sparkling deconstructionist account
of Eloise and Abelard, my laugh,
the fact I've learned to scuba dive
and mountain climb, cook *cordon vert*
without a hitch, run marathons and win,
that I'm a babe who lets you do
exactly what you want and when
who doesn't nag or hate or scorn
but keeps her dignity and more.
It will not do that I can read your thoughts,
your palm, your horoscope, your tarot and your tea,
anticipate your every move, that I can tell you
everything you'd ever want to know
about yourself or me. It will not do,
the fact I drive so fast
I make you lose your breath, that I can
squeeze my car inside the smallest space
while putting lipstick on without a smudge
that when we dance, we're never out of tune.
It will not do that I don't shout or cry or rant or plead
show you the door marked exit that I ought,
that I still kiss you till the cows come home
but still, by not being her, can't kick you
into touch. This repetition, even,
both our strange compulsions to repeat,
just will not, will not do.
And it will not do that it will not do,
that even if I were to fall in love with you again
it simply just won't do that I'm not her
and would not, do not, must not,
could not, will not, do.

Anne Rouse

ANNE ROUSE was born in 1954 in Washington DC and grew up in Virginia. She studied history at university and has since worked as a general and psychiatric nurse and an active trade unionist. Her poetry is full of wry insight and careful understatement: controlled, accurate, witty and effective language. Her first book was a Poetry Society Recommendation. She lives in London where she works as a freelance writer and mental health worker. ●

ELIZABETH ROUSE

Selection from: *Sunset Grill* (1993 Bloodaxe), *Timing* (1997 Bloodaxe).

Memo to Auden

Wystan, you got off to a wrong start,
Being neither Catholic nor tubercular,
Nor a brash, alert provincial,
But you righted like a figure-skater
And traced your syntactical curlicues
Tight and fine, to make them news.

Out of the wry side of your mouth,
You dropped a flagrant quote or two.
With my dog-eared copy for credential,
I'd like to pick a minor bone with you.
Just pretend I'm fresh at public school
And try to keep your prefectorial cool.

Do you recall the tea shop on the Broad?
You'd agreed to sit there daily
At four o'clock and dawdle, bored,
A big cat, for an exhibition fee:
Available for metric consultation
To any undergrad with nerve, or vision.

Gaping there, I lost an opportunity.
In fact I spilled Darjeeling on your shoe
(Smart Oxford brogue), and nearly missed
Watching the Jo'burg tourist corner you.
He brought a semaphoric forearm down
To shake your hand, quite heedless of your frown,

Luminous with praise,
And bombast and italicised exclaiming.
Your work had meant a lot to him, especially
That famous poem I'd re-offend by naming –
No gavel-wielding judge has ever rapped it
So sharply as Your Honour did: 'I scrapped it.'

Now to the old gnawed bone, that poetry
Makes nothing happen, the report
Of someone flatly sidelined by a war,
Who feels embarrassed holding down the fort –
Unheroically and not from duty –
Of common intellect and beauty.

The worst horrors can't be quantified,
Can't be healed, denied, forgot,
But implicit in the name of peace
Are its varied fruits, that rot
Under a swastika; its vines that die
Tied to the paling of a lie.

What is the alternative to art?
Religion of guns, guns of religion.
You know all this. You said it well,
But you have a grumpy disposition,
So I'm repeating, like an awkward kid,
What you tell us, Dad, ain't what you did.

In the careful mornings of the art
Over tonic cuppas in the lav,
Not to speak of sweaty collaboration
With Isherwood, Kallman, Britten, Strav,
You didn't do it for the bread alone:
Poets have to charm their bread from stone.

You didn't do it for the pick-up trade:
Most were arty foreigners, not rough.
You liked a wholesome share of fame,
But found the poet tag absurd enough
When talking with commercial sorts on trains.
Other professions call for verve and brains,

But you chose this one. Why?
Words are saucy, difficult but willing.
You could play boss and close the study door.
But there was another end, as thrilling
When the scholar's breath went sour:
Coaxing lines from beauty gave her power,

And this was the Holy: an act of love
To damn the bunker, damn the bomb,
And celebrate the individual life
Of myriad relations, from a room
Where the isolate voice is listened to
Through all its range, by such as you.

Let the victims, and their helpers,
And the guilty rest there for a time.
Let there be a commonality of good,
Gardens, architecture, rhyme,
That we betray by happenstance,
Forgiving airs to make us dance.

P.S. Myself I have too much to learn
Of voice and sense. You used this metre,
Don Juan too, but in our day
It's not exactly a world-beater.
Still, "subtle" can mean convoluted
And for our little chat, it suited.

Sacrificial Wolf

The careful suburban dead turn their backs
On this squat of sodden grass,
Hedged by the Finchley traffic:
The vicar poised like a prowhead
Over the shameless pit, answered
By a hectoring gull. It brings back
The afternoons in the dry houses,
The hostels and clinic waiting-rooms,
When you with the cor anglais of a shout
Parted the smokers' fug,
Flattering social workers with quotes
From Wilde or Krishnamurti –
Such was the splendour and disgrace,
That only a few of us have come to light
Our makeshift Roman candles, bitten shy:
An elegy, my friend, dear wolf,
Being just your sort of con.

A Birthday

So glad that your especial sperm
Pin-pricked your unequalled egg,
Promptly welcomed by your Mum,
Flushed and certain of your Dad's
Devotion.

So glad also the parties met,
And that a trillion forebears lived
Long enough to do the deed,
And that the first amoeba stirred
Its jelly head.

So glad that H linked twice with O,
That earth was favoured by the sun,
And that the present Total blew
From budding light, or like a bomb.

So glad you're here.

England Nil

The advance to Hamburg broke with all the plans.
Doug spelled them out in Luton Friday night.
Someone had ballsed it up. A dozen vans
Waited in convoy, ringside. Blue and white
We stumbled through. The beer
When we found it in that piss-hole of jerries
Was all we needed. Who won the war,
Anyway? Who nuked Dresden? Two fairies
Skittered behind the bar, talking Kraut
Or maybe Arabic. We clocked the poison
Smiles and chanted till the SS threw us out.
Stuttgart was a tea-party to this. One
By one they've nicked us, berserk with fear.
You've been Englished but you won't forget it, never.

Spunk Talking

When men are belligerent or crude,
it's spunk talking, it's come come up for a verbal interlude:
in your face Jack, get shagged, get screwed, get your tits out,
get him, lads, bugger that, hands off, just you try it,
you're nicked, left hook, nice one Eric, hammer hard,
shaft him, stitch that, do you want to get laid or not, red card.
Spunk speaks in gutturals, with verbs. No parentheses.
Spunk's a young con crazy to break from Alcatraz.
Sonny, you'll go feet first. So spunk has to sing,
hoarsely, the *Song of the Volga Boatmen*, *I am an Anarchist*,
the Troggs' *Wild Thing*.
Cynthia Payne said, after her researches, not to be debunked,
that men are appreciably nicer when de-spunked.
Before time began the void revolved, as smooth and bored
as an egg, when a tiny ragged crack appeared,
and the world exploded like an umpire's shout,
as the primal spunk of the cosmos bellowed OUT!

Lilies of the Field

You want corporate woman I get her for you
living doll on that billboard you like?
she got nice silicone, taped up brown eye shadow cleavage
skin by Max Factor and air brush
don't kid yourself even lights out she's a peach
spend how you like you may get her lay her
the modern world anything possible
telling your limerick on chat show
mama crying forgive her
and baby doll sucking, her big eyes on you
da da   buy buy

The Narrows

May I ask you a question?
A taxi driver to the mirror overhead.
What is there beside work and sleep?
The cab lolloped over a speed bump.

Pleasures go by, and then we're old.
We slowed to a dieselled stasis.
Cab and man were shades of black,
handing me a xeroxed sheet,

The Pursuit of Happiness.
I read it, leaning in at the meter light.
I can't remember what it said.
He was running the narrows quite alone.

I didn't have the nerve to tip.
With that muttering ease of cabs,
he drove off to confound another soul,
turning right on the station road.

Eva Salzman

MARTIN BEDDALL

EVA SALZMAN was born in 1960 in New York City, and has lived in Britain since 1985, working as a freelance writer. Her first book was a Poetry Book Society Recommendation and she received a London Arts Board New Writers Bursary in 1996. She has worked as a dancer/choreographer, out-of-print book searcher, antique market wheeler and dealer, co-editor of *The Printer's Devil* magazine and as Writer in Residence at HMP Springhill. She lives in London. ●

Selection from: *The English Earthquake* (1992 Bloodaxe), *Bargain with the Watchman* (1997 OUP).

Homesteading

It was official, in an American sort of way,
that the weather was obedient
as a dog on a leash
heeling close to each new settlement.

Ella Spawn was content for fourteen months
before she sold up for a café future in Williston.
Thereafter, Rush Blankenship takes up her written tale:
a line or two of marriage, and retail stock.
Beecher Leach of North Dakota,
remaining unmarried his entire life,
is yet remembered by some for his fried bread doughs.

See the bladeless windmill
stubbornly at attention in the hot wind
near cottonwoods ringing an empty space,
the corral's modernist geometry of sinking lines.

The buffalo wealth up the chimney for good,
now it's buffalo westerns keep you warm.

There in the central plains, one Dr Vernon
(later kicked upstairs into government)
crossed his pale white arm
over thousands of square miles, in a flash,
pronouncing them fair: *Rain follows the plow.*
The cloth got pulled out once the table was set.

What of Thorstien Odden with his Hardanger violin?
What of Gilbert Funkhouser, that jokester?
Wherefore Stella Swab and Oliver Fedge?

Still, some choked on meat,
or ditched the prairies for the North or East,
anywhere of a greener or colder complexion.

Well. No damper in your stove pipe
is as good a fame as any, mark this,
or death in a flax bin,
or even a novel method of shocking the grain.

Victorine Berquist had the last word.
To visit neighbors, then up and walk away!
No sign to her shack she'd ever thought to leave.
No sign of her was ever found.
Just a whole continent, big as this paragraph.

Bargain with the Watchman

There were two extra hooks of a worrying nature.
You'd better say it. We didn't know what we were doing.

The cratered earth, woven with roots, admitted nothing:
only later, when the pegs slid in, the canvas grew taut.

We'd browsed along the Cantal roads like butterflies,
settling lightly in a peaceful upland spot.

But the dogs barked in advance of the enemy,
the farmer riding shotgun on his tractor.

I had to strike a bargain with the watchman:
ten francs, some unwanted perfume and a burgundy kiss.

My shadow's length weighed me down like a lover,
a nightmare pressing: rose-lit arches, confetti or skin.

I was clutching the drooping tail of a pale horse
while you tethered the body, secured the spine.

Useless, I memorised the army-knife's position.
Then we drank their flaming water. Vichy.

Double Crossing
(for Jemima)

They must have known that we escaped – if only
by some slight shade across their dreams –
how our cunningly angled steps bluffed the old staircase
from its customary whinge. Then, to be home free,

we'd only have to slow the screen-door's bite,
slipping into the crickets' deafening pitch
to take that first sprint through the pines which night
unified into something we'd hardly dare enter, but did

until we'd break through the boundary of parenthood
where the moon held itself over the marshes
patiently, unnoticed by us now released into noise
and racing down the beach towards the boys.

Grandmother

The bay's little waves licked the ankles
as her poled net loitered through the warm shallows,
seaweed caught and weeping from its bent rim.
Home again, ripples from the pail told the story.

When she rolled her trousers above her aged knees,
you knew where she was headed – across the milkweed field,
into the pines, past a single cactus and the oval frame
of massed catkins, to reach the wide open bay of pure joy.

The English Earthquake

Somewhere, a cup tinkles in its saucer.
A meek 'oh my' passes down the miles
of manicured gardens, as armies rumble

the monuments of cities continents away.
The budgie chirps 'goodness' to thin air
while Bach quivers slightly and the fat roast

sways in the oven, brain-dead, but chuckling
in its oil. Such a surprise: the settling ground,
innocent with rape and mustard, groaning

under its weight of roses. The premier
sees stars, plumps her pillows for photographs.
Alas, *Watchtower* faces are falling as life goes on

and the Ex-Major winds back years to the war –
its incendiary thrill – his wife flushed
with disbelief as the earth moves unexpectedly,

the giant baby at the core of the planet
rocking its apocalyptic cradle
gently, wailing: 'Hungry, hungry, hungry.'

Ann Sansom

ANN SANSOM was born in 1951. She has written and directed two plays for Yorkshire Women Theatre and Doncaster Women's Centre. Her poetry is a heady mix of realism and an inventive narrative vision. She loves stories and these poems combine a hectic Catholic upbringing with an untrammelled imagination and the daily experiences of life in a Northern town. Ann Sansom lives and works in Sheffield. ●

Selection from: *Romance* (1994 Bloodaxe).

Voice

Call, by all means, but just once
don't use the *broken heart again* voice;
the *I'm sick to death of life and women
and romance* voice *but with a little help
I''ll try to struggle on* voice

Spare me the promise and the curse
voice, the ansafoney *Call me, please
when you get in* voice, the *nobody knows
the trouble I've seen* voice; the *I'd value
your advice* voice.

I want the how it was voice;
the *call me irresponsible but aren't I nice* voice;
the *such a bastard but I warn them in advance* voice.
The *We all have weaknesses
and mine is being wicked* voice

the *life's short and wasting time's
the only vice* voice, the *stay in touch,
but out of reach* voice. I want to hear
the *things it's better not to broach* voice
the *things it's wiser not to voice* voice.

Cross Country

It was genuine – real fox –
when she knew no better
(traps and the contemplation of pain,
the rights of the living)
and she guarded and nursed
and hugged it to her
from Darlington to Doncaster,
crooning into the collar.

At York, in the five-minute break,
she ran through the sleet –
shouldering the coat, a big soft sleeping child,
the sleek inlay spotted
and starred with wet, the tie ribbons trailing –
and came back breathless, scenting
the compartment with musk and chocolate.

There was an oval compact,
steel and red enamel that she opened,
scowled into, and snapped shut, satisfied.
And he was talking, giving her
the benefit of his philosophy.
The secret of happiness.
Own nothing. Want nothing.

Backing in past St George's,
the snow circled, settling briefly
shifting on the dark; the lights
in the goods yard, the sidings,
slowing, *We are now approaching...*
And in the three minute tunnel
he told her, All journeys end.
And that is the beauty of them.

Does this coat have Buddha-Life?
Open it. Here in the hem,
eleven flat lead weights.
A master number. Count them.

There is suffering, my dear,
and there is non-attachment. Allow me.
Seven linings. Brown silk on grey silk
on unbleached linen. Reach past
these layers of nylon, hessian,
netting, the pulse in your fingertips.
Feel. The moist suede innard of the animal.

From the moment I picked up your book

'From the moment I picked up your book,
I was convulsed. One day I intend to read it.'
        GROUCHO MARX

I know you. I recognise the stumbling sway,
the way that you choose me. The full length
of an empty carriage and you choose me.
And you choose wrong. I'm busy here,

a *Sunday Sport* left on the seat – AMAZING
STONE AGE WOMAN FOUND ALIVE IN CAVE,
ASTOUNDING SEXY FEATS OF NEW AGE MAN –
Persuasion still unopened on the table,

the Walkman sizzling between two stations.
I'm occupied, engaged, but you move in
and with one swipe, clear off the debris,
spread your big white man-size hanky.

A tablecloth? And you intend to dine, perhaps?
A candelabra from your pocket, a violin, a rose
offered between here and Leeds? How dare you
interrupt a woman with two hundred pages

left to read, a woman who if you weren't here
could lie back with her feet up on the seat.
All right. I've been on trains before.
I know some people can be rocked

beyond restraint, made bold in transit,
and some will offer up the underside
of what they do in dreams and some
can't wait to show the things they do,

or want to do at home. And some.
I wonder, vaguely, where I'm going now,
where you are coming from...
Don't be deceived. This is not fear.

I shake because I'm venomous.
I'm white with murderous disdain.
I am this wall, this luggage rack, this door.
I am not here. And you are not

my final fellow traveller.
You're almost out of sight, midway
between the table and the vacant seat
and I repress the reflex, the sharp instinct –

no lady ever kicks a kneeling man
nor dares offend a crawling one.
I focus on the book, concentrate,
her carriage and deportment were quiet...

You reappear, a flushed and happy conjuror,
presenting, just between us, first one naked foot
she had been forced into prudence in her youth,
and then, in time, the other

she learned romance as she grew older.
The soles are very clean, almost unused.
You're barefoot, harmless. Who could take offence?
I'm calm. You're simply ignorant of rules.

But pedicures are always serious;
you frown to get it right. Perfectionist.
When every toe-nail's sliced
you scoop the creamy crescent clippings,

reach up, release them from the hanky,
fluttering from the window, sparse confetti.
A neat man. Tidy. Every action slow.
Your smile. The way you roll your socks

to a soft fist, slide it in your pocket.
Your smile. Your finger on the blade,
the way that you retract it. Your smile.
I remain polite. When you stand up

I nod to your *goodnight.*
And when you've really gone
I close the book
on all the times I had the sense

to cut and run and froze instead,
but paid for it in buckets of cold sweat.
This is where I dip my finger in
and draw the real hard line. I'm giving up

my corner seat, my common courtesy
to men who groom themselves
with Stanley knives, to gentlemen
who will not let me read in peace on trains.

Romance

This is how he made her fall
in love with him. This is the tale
he always tells when he feels like talking.
The long one with the happy ending.

How he came by his sons, his daughters
our bold fathers, our pretty mothers
and the increasing shifting numbers of us.
This is where he finally won the prize

he wanted more than anything. She comes in,
her arms full, heading for the kitchen.
Awhile here, girl. I'm after telling them about
the night at Gallagher's I played the flute.

Now, surely to God, you remember that?
He winks to us, in no doubt. *I remember it –*
not breaking her long stride, smiling – *Indeed I do.*
And a terrible thing it was, if I may say so now.

He waits till she's gone. Remember this.
You never touch a Mayo tinker's bitch.
Nor any kind of laughing brazen
red-haired hard-of-hearing woman.

Susan Wicks

DAVID MARKSON

SUSAN WICKS was born in 1947. She grew up in Kent and was educated at the universities of Hull and Sussex. She has taught in France and Ireland and works as a part-time tutor for the University of Kent. Her poetry is deft, precise and surprising – homing in on apparently ordinary moments which are transformed in her hands to become revelatory. Her third collection, *The Clever Daughter*, was a Poetry Book Society Choice. ●

Selection from: *Singing Underwater* (1992), *Open Diagnosis* (1994), *The Clever Daughter* (1996): all Faber.

The Clever Daughter
(after a misericord in Worcester Cathedral)

For six hundred years I have travelled
to meet my father. *Neither walking nor riding,*
I have carried your heartbeat to him
carefully, to the sound of singing,
my right hand growing to horn.

Your head droops in a stain of windows
as we come closer. The man who made us –
hare and girl – will barely recognise
the lines his blade left: six centuries
have fused us to a single figure.

Clothed and unclothed, we shall reach him,
netted at his cold feet. But as he unwraps us,
my cloak-threads snagging and breaking,
I shall release you, your pent flutter
of madness. And we shall see you

run from his hands and vanish,
your new zigzag opening the cornfield
like the path of lovers, the endless journey
shaken from your long ears, my gift to him
given and yet not given.

Moderato
(after Marguerite Duras)

My child never played the piano.
It was the clarinet mostly.
You can't count a recorder.
And no escaping boat crossed the window
from frame to horizon.
She played in a pink-gold room under the lamp,
and the flowered curtains remained closed.

There was no murder in a French café.
No crowd gathered.
Our crimes were quite bloodless.
No one was escorted to the closed van,
desire still smeared on their faces.
For us it took somewhat longer than a week.

But there was a magnolia tree, certainly.
The smell of flowers was all down the hill.
I didn't actually press them to my bosom.
My bosom isn't of that sort.
But I did have one in my pocket for a while,
pink and white with brown edges.
And if you had offered me a knife
I'd have slit my throat gladly,
and you might have tried dipping your fastidious
prick briefly in the hole.

Buying Fish

I am one of you, though you do not
know it. We are all hesitant, we are all
gentle and elderly. Together
we point and stutter. Our string bags wait
for wet parcels, gape to receive

the same slippery gift. Tonight we shall all
search our mouths for bones,
as the fragile skeletons
are picked clean, discarded, wrapped in plastic
to cheat the rough tongues of cats. I am
one of you. Watch me buy a thin fillet
of plaice for my single serving, drop keys, fumble
the change. I can beg as well as you
for a few sprigs of sour parsley. I can look
a whole slab of rainbow
trout straight in the eye.

Protected Species

My parents' papers lie round me
bundled in boxes, the lids dotted
with the droppings of bats, the names
faded, too faint for a stranger's eye
to interpret. I pull, and the perished bands
snap into dust, a grey sheet blisters
with flying fragments. *Joy darling*:
in the roof his circling voice
transmits its high-pitched signal
to her voice. My parents' wartime letters,
starred with small explosions, have flown
great distances, their words blanching
on the page, their steady messages
bringing the world back
to an attic where protected species
hang upside-down, flexing
their claws in a dream of darkness,
shaking their skinny wings.

Voice

In the garden shed, among flower-pots,
his words explode into her:
You fucking cow, you came out here
just to... all you fucking wanted...
As I peg out the laundry
I hear him still haranguing
silence, her answers whispered so low
they could be absence. He pauses
to pant and breathe and she
emerges, head bowed, carrying a teacup.

Later I hear them in their adjacent
bedroom, their old bed-springs
creaking, his spent mouth finally
quiet, as a new voice gurgles and rises
in her throat, calling
like a muezzin or a goatherd,
bridging the strange intervals.

Rain Dance

This is how they make rain, the raw
repeated drumbeat of two pulses, this green gauze
that settles on their skin and gleams
like light on water. This is how he creates her,
fluid as green drops fusing
on new growth, bent to this holy posture
of damage, her raised green satin instep
stroking her own right cheek, as he still turns her,
twists her as if through creepers,
this green sediment of branches
layered on air, as his taut body
dances on hers. They will reach the light soon. He bends her
this way and that, her head flips backwards
into his darkness, her neck surely broken.

Her two legs split perfectly open
like roots. There is moisture
between them now as he drags her, wood
rasping her inside thighs. The rapt watchers
gasp with her pain, if she could only
feel it. Curved for his blessing,
her skin glistens as he still strokes her
like a green pot into being
on this wheel of rhythms
where they are gods, unmindful now of bodies,
our single-jointed history
of breakage, and the sweat runs off them.

Joy

The authorities do not permit us
to take pictures: this dance is ephemeral
as sex or April dogwoods, the pink-skirted
ripple of her body, her emaciated
trunk gleaming, the snapped wishbone
of her thigh sparking light. The pink wit
of her flexed foot stirs us unaccountably
to laughter. This is the dancer's way, this meeting
of tangent bodies, this cool coffee
at café tables, the momentary pink stasis
of words, the fading blossom
drifted from chestnuts. This must be spring,
her limbs' own joy, as his arms lift her,
carry her on his shoulders
into darkness. We may not take pictures.
We look and look, drinking
the small death of each step, each contact
of flesh on sliding flesh, the precise circles
of what we crave, the gasps that express us.

ALSO AVAILABLE FROM BLOODAXE:

Kissing a Bone

by MAURA DOOLEY

POETRY BOOK SOCIETY RECOMMENDATION

Maura Dooley's poetry is remarkable for embracing both lyricism and political consciousness, for its fusion of head and heart. These qualities have won her wide acclaim. Helen Dunmore (in *Poetry Review*) admired her 'sharp and forceful' intelligence. Adam Thorpe praised her ability 'to enact and find images for complex feelings... Her poems have both great delicacy and an undeniable toughness... she manages to combine detailed domesticity with lyrical beauty, most perfectly in the metaphor of memory' (*Literary Review*). In *Kissing a Bone*, her second book-length collection, Maura Dooley's focus has broadened. In a landscape stretching from Tranquillity Base to Crossmaglen, via the Northern Line and the Berlin Wall, memory and photography, love and death, are captured through the imperfect lens of history.

Classical Women Poets

translated by JOSEPHINE BALMER

Fragmented and forgotten, the women poets of ancient Greece and Rome have long been overlooked by translators and scholars. Yet to Antipater of Thessalonica, writing in the first century AD, these were the 'earthly Muses' whose poetic skills rivalled those of their heavenly namesakes: 'Their songs delight the gods...and mortals too for all time.' Today only a fraction of their work survives – lyrical, witty, often innovative, and always moving – offering surprising insights into the closed world of women in antiquity, from childhood friendships through love affairs and marriage to motherhood and bereavement. Josephine Balmer's translations breathe new life into long-lost works by over a dozen poets from early Greece to the late Roman empire, including Sappho, Corinna, Erinna and Sulpicia, as well as inscriptions, folk-songs and even graffiti. Each poet is introduced by a brief bibliographical note, and where necessary unfamiliar mythological or historical references are explained. *Classical Women Poets* is a companion volume to Josephine Balmer's edition *Sappho: Poems & Fragments*, also published by Bloodaxe.

Consorting with Angels
Modern Women Poets
by DERYN-REES JONES

Until recently, women's poetry has been at best sidelined and at worst forgotten. In this pioneering study, Deryn Rees-Jones argues that the poetic traditions of the 20th century must be radically rethought in the light of the formal and thematic experimentation of three generations of women poets. Establishing a lineage of women poets, from the more well-known work of Edith Sitwell, Stevie Smith, Elizabeth Jennings, Elizabeth Bishop, Sylvia Plath and Anne Sexton, to the equally exciting work of Sheila Wingfield, and contemporary poets such as Jo Shapcott, Gwyneth Lewis, Grace Nichols, Carol Ann Duffy, Selima Hill and Medbh McGuckian, Rees-Jones sets out to show the vitality and ingenuity of women's poetry in Britain and America this century.

Sixty Women Poets
edited by LINDA FRANCE
POETRY BOOK SOCIETY SPECIAL COMMENDATION

This anthology charts the irrepressible growth and flowering of women's poetry in Britain and Ireland over the past two decades. 'Relaxed, confident, commonsensical, humorous and a triumphant success...the guiding force for Linda France is of "women being positive, creative and in control of their own lives" ' – PETER FORBES, *Guardian*. 'She has almost unfailingly chosen well: this is simply an excellent collection of recent poetry' – NEIL POWELL, *PN Review*. 'This is full-bodied, full-blooded stuff...there's ambivalence and unease as well as celebration' – SUZI FEAY, *Time Out*.

The Bloodaxe Book of Contemporary Women Poets
edited by JENI COUZYN

Large selections – with essays on their work – by eleven poets: Sylvia Plath, Stevie Smith, Kathleen Raine, Fleur Adcock, Anne Stevenson, Elizabeth Jennings, Denise Levertov, Elaine Feinstein, Jenny Joseph, Ruth Fainlight and Jeni Couzyn. *Illustrated*.

WRITERS PUBLISHED BY

BLOODAXE BOOKS

FLEUR ADCOCK
ANNA AKHMATOVA
GILLIAN ALLNUTT
MONIZA ALVI
ANNEMARIE AUSTIN
JOSEPHINE BALMER
ELIZABETH BARTLETT
CONNIE BENSLEY
ROBYN BOLAM
KARIN BOYE
JEAN 'BINTA' BREEZE
ELEANOR BROWN
INGER CHRISTENSEN
POLLY CLARK
JULIA COPUS
JENI COUZYN
AMANDA DALTON
IMTIAZ DHARKER
KATIE DONOVAN
MAURA DOOLEY
FREDA DOWNIE
HELEN DUNMORE
LAURIS EDMOND
MENNA ELFYN
RUTH FAINLIGHT
CAROLYN FORCHÉ
TUA FORSSTRÖM
LINDA FRANCE
TESS GALLAGHER
ELIZABETH GARRETT
PAMELA GILLILAN
JANE GRIFFITHS
MAGGIE HANNAN
JACKIE HARDY
TRACEY HERD
RITA ANN HIGGINS
SELIMA HILL
JANE HOLLAND
FRANCES HOROVITZ
FRIEDA HUGHES
IOANA IERONIM

HELEN IVORY
KATHLEEN JAMIE
JENNY JOSEPH
JACKIE KAY
DENISE LEVERTOV
GWYNETH LEWIS
JOANNE LIMBURG
MARION LOMAX
EDNA LONGLEY
KATHLEEN McCRACKEN
MAIRI MacINNES
MARAM AL-MASSRI
ESTHER MORGAN
JULIE O'CALLAGHAN
CAITRÍONA O'REILLY
RUTH PADEL
CLARE POLLARD
KATRINA PORTEOUS
DEBORAH RANDALL
DERYN REES-JONES
ANNE ROUSE
CAROL RUMENS
TRACY RYAN
ANN SANSOM
SAPPHO
CAROLE SATYAMURTI
GJERTRUD SCHNACKENBERG
OLIVE SENIOR
JO SHAPCOTT
ELENA SHVARTS
EDITH SÖDERGRAN
ESTA SPALDING
PAULINE STAINER
ANNE STEVENSON
PIA TAFDRUP
MARINA TSVETAYEVA
MIRJAM TUOMINEN
CHASE TWICHELL
LILIANA URSU
CHRISTIANIA WHITEHEAD
CLAIR WILLS

Bloodaxe Books is Britain's premier poetry publisher, bringing out more new poetry books – and more women poets – than any other British imprint. For a complete Bloodaxe catalogue, please write to:
Bloodaxe Books Ltd, Highgreen, Tarset, Northumberland NE48 1RP.